The Amazing Jamnasium

A Playful Companion to **Together in Rhythm**

Kalani

Alfred Publishing Co., Inc.
Alfred.com

ISBN 0-7390-3625-4 (Book and CD)

Contents

About the Enhanced CD

The Amazing Jamnasium CD doubles as a fun multimedia learning tool that works on any Windows-compatible or Macintosh computer. Play the CD in a standard CD player to access the five rhythm tracks listed in the **Grooves to Drum By** section. Place the CD in your computer to enjoy watching video footage of many of the rhythm games.

About the Author

Kalani is one of the world's foremost drum circle facilitators, a keynote presenter, trainer, accomplished studio and touring percussionist, world-music composer, educator, and award-winning author. His personable, down-to-earth style inspires participants to celebrate life though music and helps them to develop better relationships with their fellow students, co-workers, families and friends.

Kalani has received numerous awards for his work as a drum circle facilitator, percussion clinician, performer and author. He presents workshops and seminars for the International Music Products Association (NAMM), the Percussive Arts Society, the National Association of Music Educators (MENC), the American Orff-Schulwerk Association, the American Music Therapy Association, the American Music Conference, the Los Angeles Philharmonic, the National Academy of Recording Arts and Sciences (the Grammy Foundation), and numerous other state and regional music education organizations.

He is the founder and director of Drumlesson.com, an educational drumming website that has been featured by the *New York Times* and *CNN Live*. He is the artistic director of World Rhythms drum and dance programs, which preserve and promote music, dance and cross-cultural appreciation through educational resources and experiences (DrumCamp.com).

Kalani is a featured musician on recordings from Disney, Warner Brothers, Tri-Star, Paramount, the Nature Company, and Jim Hensen Records. He has performed and recorded with such music legends as Kenny Loggins, David Sanborn, Max Roach, Barry Manilow, Vic Damone, John Mayall, Chante Moore, Dr. John, Suzanne Ciani, and Melissa Manchester, and he is the featured percussionist on the *Yanni: Live at the Acropolis* video and CD. He has released two CDs of original music, *Pangea* and *Insights*, and has produced a number of instructional books and DVDs.

Kalani is an intuitive musical coach who helps people from all walks of life to learn, work, and live together in rhythm. He works closely with several of the music industry's top companies as an instrument and program design consultant. A certified Orff-Schulwerk educator, he travels throughout the world as a drum circle facilitator, music educator, performer, presenter and trainer, and his programs are well-represented in music stores and educational institutions. He is a pioneer in the field of combining music and wellness, and has developed strategies that are used in health clubs and schools to promote better health, teamwork and camaraderie.

Acknowledgments

I extend my heartfelt thanks to the following people for their contributions, time and attention to this book:

My Orff Schulwerk instructors Doug Goodkin, Konnie Saliba, Sofia Lopez-Ibor, James Harding, Will Salmon.

Music educators who helped "road test" much of this material: Brenda Williams (Rockvale Elementary School, Rockvale, Tennessee); Joanne Cinti (William Street School, Lancaster, New York); Karen Williamson (Prairie Mountain School, Eugene, Oregon); Martha Evans Osborne (Patterson Elementary, Hillsboro, Oregon); Debbie Fahmie (Cypress Elementary, Kissimmee, Florida); Veronika Schultz (Lincoln Elementary School, Riverton, Wyoming); Kay Lovingood (Martinez Elementary, Martinez, Georgia); Joan Eckroth-Riley (Northridge Elementary, Bismarck, North Dakota); Sue Michiels (traveling teacher, Los Angeles, California); Margaret Jerz (Evergreen Elementary, Wasau, Wisconsin).

Gregg Charron and Gretchen Neilson from the Los Angeles Philharmonic's Partnership in Education Program.

Music therapists Michael Marcionetti and Barry Bernstein, and my training partner Janet Marinaccio.

Kelly Weaver for researching and building instruments, and C.J. Hansen for modeling the homemade instruments.

Dave Black, Kim Kasabian, Kate Westin, Andrew Surmani, and everyone at Alfred Publishing. (Alfred.com)

Introduction

What Is a *Jamnasium*?

jam: To play music in an improvised way, often in a group.

gymnasium: A place equipped for physical exercise or training.

Jamnasium: A place for musical exploration, group activities and creative expression.

A Jamnasium[1] is a place where creativity is valued over conformity and where working together to reach the goal **is** the goal. A Jamnasium offers many possibilities for collaboration, rewards cooperation over competition, and celebrates the personal diversities that help create rich and rewarding experiences. A Jamnasium is a place of joy, unlimited expression, and freedom from judgment. It is where people learn how to listen, to share their spirit in a way that is right for them, and discover how their unique gifts contribute to a community that is playing, working, and living together in rhythm.

As an educator, therapist, or music facilitator, you're sure to appreciate the value of compelling activities that allow participants to engage one another in ways that bring out their best and leave them with a sense of community, accomplishment, and uplifted spirits. Group drumming activities and rhythm games have long been praised for their ability to help people develop a variety of skills and positive life habits, from physical coordination and mathematical concepts to social skills like teamwork and the celebration of diversity. This special collection of curriculum-ready music-based games, activities, and resources is designed to help music facilitators infuse their programs with fun, creativity, and rhythm.

What Does a Jamnasium Offer?

Jamnasium activities help participants to

- develop social skills such as listening, support and sharing;
- improvise as a group to solve problems and create meaningful experiences;
- develop a variety of musical and movement skills that support the National Standards for Arts Education;
- gain an appreciation for diversity and each participant's unique gifts;
- understand mathematical concepts and how to recognize patterns;
- reduce the effects of stress and enjoy participating in a social activity.

Use this material to develop programs for the following:

- Music education
- Music therapy
- Team building
- Health and fitness
- Community development

What Is the Best Way to Present This Material?

While this book may be used on its own, these games and activities are most effectively presented using the Drum Circle Music™ (DCM) approach to music facilitation. If you haven't already done so, I encourage you to read my book *Together in Rhythm: A Facilitator's Guide to Drum Circle Music* for a comprehensive overview of the DCM approach that will provide you with a solid foundation in the art of facilitation. Practicing the Drum Circle Music approach can help you become a better communicator, presenter, and facilitator. If you're like most people, you'll have other questions that extend beyond the presentation of these activities such as, *What is the best way to organize an event? What are the best ways to deal with problems that come up? Which instruments are best for certain populations/ activities? How do I encourage participation without being controlling? How do I create an effective program? How can I be more effective and place less pressure on myself at the same time?* If you're looking for answers to these and other questions, you can find them in *Together in Rhythm.*

---

[1] *Jamnasium* is a trademark of Kalani Music. Commercial use of this mark without written consent from Kalani Music is prohibited. *Boomwhackers* is a registered trademark of Whacky Music, Inc. *Joia Tubes* is a trademark of Unity Through Percussion. *Rainbow Hand Drums* is a trademark of Peripole-Bergerault, Inc.

All About Rhythm

Counting Basics

If you're not familiar with reading and counting music, take a couple of moments to review this exercise. Most of the examples in this book are based on simple rhythms that use both *downbeats* (on the pulse) and *upbeats* (notes between the downbeats).

Simple pulse counting (downbeats)

Beat number	1	2	3	4
Step R=right L=left	R	L	R	L
Say	"one	two	three	four"

Adding upbeats to the downbeats:

Beat number	1	+	2	+	3	+	4	+
Step/Clap	R	clap	L	clap	R	clap	L	clap
Say	"one	and	two	and	three	and	four	and"

Developing Rhythmic Feel & Coordination

Vocal Percussion

I often guide a group from instruments to vocal percussion and back again to add variety and help them feel the rhythms from the inside out. Vocal percussion jams can also bring out the creativity in the group because the participants can all "play" these sounds and don't have the technical barriers that can be associated with playing instruments.

In the Kodály (koh-DYE) method, students use various sounds such as *Toe*, *Ta* and *Ti* to represent beats and subdivisions:

Ti = Eighth Note .....♪...(½ a beat, either downbeat or upbeat)

Ta = Quarter Note ...♩....(1 full beat)

Toe = Half Note.......♩....(2 full beats)

Example:

1	+	2	+	3	+	4	+	1	+	2	+	3	+	4	+
Ta		Ta		Ti	Ti	Ta		Ti	Ti	Ta		Toe			
1/4		1/4		1/8	1/8	1/4		1/8	1/8	1/4		1/2			

Other subjects for vocal percussion jams include the following:

- People's names
- Proper nouns (places, things, etc.)
- Rhymes, chants, and poetry
- Statements, stories, and affirmations

Body Percussion

Use body percussion activities to help develop rhythmic concepts and physical coordination.

The four primary body percussion sounds are *snap*, *clap*, *pat*, and *stamp* (or *stomp*).

1	+	2	+	3	+	4	+	1	+	2	+	3	+	4	+
Snap	Snap	Snap		Snap	Snap	Snap		Clap	Clap		Clap	Clap		Clap	

1	+	2	+	3	+	4	+	1	+	2	+	3	+	4	+
Pat	Pat	Pat	Pat	Pat	Pat	Pat	Pat	Stamp		Stamp		Stamp			

Process

1. Introduce each 4–beat group on its own.

   Note: Repeated sounds are played with alternating movements (right–left–right–left).

2. Combine them in groups of two, then all four in sequence.

3. Try it as a *round* by grouping four sections of the circle and starting each section four beats apart.

   Tip: Try matching vocal percussion with the above example. Use a different vocal sound for each body percussion sound.

Body Percussion & Voice Together

This is an example of two simple body percussion rhythms (one with three notes and one with five) that can be layered together to produce an interesting poly-rhythmic effect. Each pattern is reinforced with a vocal sound.

Note that both phrases are six beats long.

Beat	1	+	2	+	3	+	4	+	5	+	6	+
1	Ta				Ta				Ta			
	Clap	Pat	Pat		Clap	Pat	Pat		Clap	Pat	Pat	
2	Toe						Toe					
	Clap	Pat	Pat	Stamp	Stamp		Clap	Pat	Pat	Stamp	Stamp	

Process

1. Introduce and repeat rhythm no. 1 until everyone has joined in. Say "Ta" on the first note of every phrase.

2. Introduce and repeat rhythm no. 2 until everyone has joined in. Say "Toe" on the first note of every phrase.

3. Cue half the group to stop and repeat step 1 with that half so both rhythms are being played together.

4. When ready, have the two groups switch parts.

   Option: Have students sing the vocals on specific pitches, for example, a third or fourth apart.

Tips for Group Drumming

Rhythm-based activities involve listening skills and coordination. Because rhythm is the part of music that pertains to forward motion, we must always do our best to maximize the participants' potential for success by providing tools and techniques that will make it easy for them to move forward together.

Have a few key percussion parts.

Have someone keep a steady beat on a cowbell or woodblock. Remind shaker and rattle players to use alternating motions to keep patterns flowing and easy to play. Encourage simplicity and repetition.

Have bass drums support the pulse.

When using more than one bass drum, ask players to play complementary parts (ones that balance each other by alternating or overlapping). Suggest they accent the strong beats, e.g., the first and third of every four.

Keep additional percussion parts simple.

Adding the smaller percussion instruments creates a "rhythmic grid" that will complement the pulse and help glue all the other parts together. Encourage patterns that are simple. *It's a gift to be simple!*

Add the hand drums last.

Because hand drums are the only instrument group that is primarily played with both hands, parts can end up being very busy. Beginning group rhythms with all the other instruments provides a solid foundation for the hand drummers that may encourage them to play simple parts with more built-in space.

Grooves to Drum By

Some of the best music happens when people make up their own rhythms. However, there are times when it's appropriate to provide a few parts for people to play. These include educational settings where the facilitator is in fact the music teacher, drum circles where most if not all of the participants are total beginners and may be looking for some guidance, and activities where the rhythms have special functions such as to emulate the feel of a certain style such as Brazilian or African. The following rhythm arrangements feature simple parts that you can use as inspiration for your drum circle, music classes or movement activities. Each arrangement is made up of five different rhythm patterns for the following instrument categories; bass drum, hand drum, wood sound, rattle/shaker, and bell. I've made sure to include a member from each of the four main timbre groups (plus bass drums) so each rhythm represents a full spectrum of diverse sounds.

Legend		
*	=	High/(muted surdo) tone
•	=	Low/(open surdo) tone
(•)	=	Accent

 **Track 1**

MM=130

	1	+	2	+	3	+	4	+	1	+	2	+	3	+	4	+
Cowbell	•		*		•		*	*	•		*		•		*	*
Rattle	•		•		•		•		•		•		•		•	
Woodblock	•	•		•		•	•		•	•		•		•	•	
Conga	•		*	*	*		•	•	•		*		•	•	•	•
Dundun	•				•		•		•				•		•	

Celebration Circle   Track 2

MM=150

	1	+	2	+	3	+	4	+	1	+	2	+	3	+	4	+
Cowbell	•		•		•				•		•		•			
Tambourine	(•)	•	•	•	(•)	•	•	•	(•)	•	•	•	(•)	•	•	•
Woodblock	•		•	•		•			•		•	•		•		
Jembe	•		*	*		*	*	*	•			•		*	*	
Dundun	•				•				•				•			

The Rio Thang   Track 3

MM=160

	1	+	2	+	3	+	4	+	1	+	2	+	3	+	4	+
Agogo	•		*		•		*		•	*		*	•		*	
Shaker	(•)	•	•	(•)	(•)	•	•	(•)	(•)	•	•	(•)	(•)	•	•	(•)
Tone Block	•		•			•		•		•			•		•	
Conga	*		•	•	•		*	*	*		•	•	•		*	
Surdo	*				•				*				•			

Village Life   Track 4

Note: *This example has 6 beats in a phrase (often referred to as $\frac{6}{8}$ meter) instead of 4. Because each beat in this rhythm is equal in length to one-half beat in the previous examples, no upbeats (+'s) are used in the notation. The primary pulse is felt on "1" and "4" of each phrase.*

MM=100

	1	2	3	4	5	6	1	2	3	4	5	6
Gankogui	•		*	*		•	•		*		•	
Shekere	•			•			•			•		
Tone Block	•	•	•				•					
Jembe	•		*	*	•	•	•		*	*	•	•
Dundun	•			•			•			•		

Caribbeing   Track 5

MM=170

	1	+	2	+	3	+	4	+	1	+	2	+	3	+	4	+
Cowbell	•		*	*	•		*	*	•		*		•		*	*
Cabasa	•		•	•		•	•		•		•	•		•	•	
Clave	•			•			•				•		•			
Conga	•		*	*	•	•	*	*	•		*	*	•	•	*	*
Surdo	*			•			*		*			•			*	

Ways You Can Use the Music Tracks

Play Along

Play these tracks for people as they arrive at your event to help them get in the mood to make music together. You can also use them to jumpstart a drum circle, inviting your participants to play along. The tracks serve to provide participants with a steady beat and offer some rhythmic ideas they can use in their own playing. Encourage them to match some of the parts they hear in the music. Fade out the music and let your group take it away!

Dance/Move Along

Play this music for your movement classes. Invite students to create their own movements to the different rhythms or teach your own group or partner dance. Each rhythm has a specific feel. Ask students to move to each track in different ways and describe what they were feeling at the time. What places, animals or themes does the music bring to mind? Have them choose a track and present their dance for the rest of the group.

Practice Partner

Learn the rhythms from these grooves and share them with your participants. Because each track lasts for eight minutes, they make great practice partners. Try improvising over the music or simply match a part and stay in the groove. Make up your own complementary parts, melodic accompaniment or songs.

Learning Tip: Present all of the above rhythms as body percussion before playing them on the instruments. Substitute snaps for the bell part, high claps for the shaker or rattle part, low claps for the wood part, patting for the drum part, and stamping (stepping) for the bass drum part. First, have the whole group play each part one at a time, then divide into groups playing different patterns, and then play as a canon or rhythm round. This may help to facilitate learning the rhythms, and it's fun!

Creating a Pocket

A *pocket* is the place in time where everyone's hands and hearts are lined up, where you feel the power of unity and the magic of synergy. Falling into a groove is not just about *entrainment* (two or more bodies traveling at the same speed and direction), it's about an agreement between the participants to come together to create community music. When everyone's parts fit together in perfect alignment, the music is self-supporting. As a facilitator, your role is often to find ways to help your people identify the pulse, hear it clearly, and discover ways of playing along that feel right for them. You can do this by helping them to play simple parts, focusing their attention to a supportive instrument (bass drum, shaker, bell), playing a steady pulse on an instrument that is easy to hear, and emphasizing *listening* as much as, or more than, you emphasize *playing*. Remind your students that playing music is not a competition to see who can play the fastest or loudest, but rather an opportunity to listen to one another, play together, and work as a team.

About the Games and Activities

The following games and activities are designed to be fun and challenging cooperative learning opportunities for people of all ages. They are flexible, adaptable and expandable, offering many possible means of transporting a group through many rhythmic adventures. Which games are suited for what age groups and how to modify them for special populations I leave up to the facilitators, as only they will know how to best serve the needs of their groups. For example, a music therapist may choose to simplify an activity for a group of developmentally disabled adults, while a teacher may make the same activity more challenging for a group of advanced students. Movements may be scaled down for a group of elderly folk, though in a school program for children, a recreational activity director may add to the physical element. (See the Quick Reference Chart on page 50 to help determine which games may be best suited for your particular groups and goals.) Although I use the term "students" in many of the descriptions, the term "participants" could just as easily be used for general applications, or "clients" could be used for music therapy applications.

Note: The games are listed in general order of complexity, with the easier ones first and the more challenging ones last.

I have personally presented these activities with children as well as adults. They can be used in any of your programs whether the overall goal is to promote education, team-building, appreciation of diversity, physical well-being, mental/emotional health, or just plain fun. All of these activities can be used to develop fine and gross motor skills, attention span, leadership skills, teamwork skills, cognitive skills, communication skills, social skills, self-esteem, reality orientation, taking turns, following directions, creative self-expression, and modeling behaviors. I encourage you to experiment with and expand on the process and elements of each game, presenting them in your own way and in your own style. These are only starting points from which to launch your group's imagination. Have fun with them, and see where they grow!

Important note: While I have worked to provide a clear process for presenting these activities, note that the main goal of each activity is not to "perform" them perfectly, and that you don't have to follow my steps exactly in order to help students benefit from the activities. I mention this because sometimes, as teachers, we may feel that if we're not "playing the game properly" then we're not fulfilling our role. This is simply not the case. The goal in presenting each game is to encourage personal connections, foster creativity, raise self-esteem, and help students learn how to work together. The game is simply the vehicle that gets them to reach that goal. As long as your standards for creativity and personal growth are being met, whichever way you choose to play a game is the "right" way. In many cases, your students will change or add to a way a game is played. Hurray! This is a sign that they feel involved, empowered and excited about the activity. When everyone in a group feels valued and empowered to shape their experience, a community is created.

The elements of each game and activity are presented in the following order:

1. Time span
2. Instruments
3. Other materials
4. Focus
5. National Standards for Music Education (NS)
6. Multiple Intelligences (MI)
7. Music Therapy applications (MT)
8. Preparation
9. Process
10. Extension
11. Discussion

Time Span

This is a very basic, ballpark figure of how long the core activity described in "Process" usually takes the average group. Characteristics of the group (such as the age of the participants) will often determine if a longer or shorter time frame should be expected. This information is provided as a *guideline only* to help facilitators quickly distinguish longer activities from shorter ones and should be helpful when putting a program together or for any situation in which time is a factor. It is not meant as a parameter to be followed.

Instruments

General types of instruments are provided to allow the greatest flexibility for each activity. Specific suggestions are provided for instruments that work particularly well.

Other Materials

If any items other than instruments are necessary, they are listed here.

Focus

These are the abilities and areas of learning that a given activity will primarily affect. They are provided to further characterize each activity for the facilitator so that appropriate choices can be made based on goals and desired outcome.

National Standards for Music Education (NS)

Performing, creating and responding to music are the fundamental music processes in which humans engage. Students, particularly those in grades K–4, learn by doing. Singing, playing instruments, moving to music, and creating music enables them to acquire musical skills and knowledge that can be developed in no other way. Learning to read and notate music gives them a skill with which to explore music independently and with others. Listening to, analyzing, and evaluating music are important building blocks of musical learning. Furthermore, to participate fully in a diverse, global society, students must understand their own historical and cultural heritage and that of others within their communities and beyond. Because music is a basic expression of human culture, every student should have access to a balanced, comprehensive, and sequential program of study in music. These standards outline the basic qualities of any complete music program. You can use them as a guide when creating curriculum; however; they may be best thought of as a starting point rather than as a goal.

Standards[2]

1. Singing, alone and with others, a varied repertoire of music.

2. Performing on instruments, alone and with others, a varied repertoire of music.

3. Improvising melodies, variations, and accompaniments.

4. Composing and arranging music within specified guidelines.

5. Reading and notating music.

6. Listening to, analyzing, and describing music.

7. Evaluating music and music performances.

8. Understanding relationships between music, the other arts, and disciplines outside the arts.

9. Understanding music in relation to history and culture.

Multiple Intelligences (MI)

Developing a deeper understanding and awareness of personal and group dynamics requires that we first acknowledge that everyone in the world thinks, learns and communicates in different ways (hurray for that!) In his book *Frames of Mind: The Theory of Multiple Intelligences* (Basic Books, 1983), Howard Gardner presented the idea of *multiple intelligences*. His design of human learning styles and ways of thinking is comprised of at least eight separate but interconnected intelligences that, together, form the basis for a multi-dimensional perspective of human cognition. Brief descriptions of these eight intelligences are outlined below.

Verbal/Linguistic: The ability to think and communicate in words and text. Authors, poets, journalists, speakers and educators often exhibit high degrees of linguistic intelligence. In musical terms, this intelligence may manifest itself as the ability to recall or create lyrics to songs or to learn lyrics quickly.

Mathematical/Logical: The ability to calculate, quantify and consider hypotheses based on information, numbers and scientific laws of nature. Scientists, accountants, engineers and programmers must possess this intelligence. In musical terms, it may present itself through an ability to conceive of musical form and arrangement, or as an advanced understanding of harmonic and rhythmic relationships.

Visual/Spatial: The ability to think in three dimensions and perceive external and internal imagery; also, to create, transform and identify images and objects and to navigate pathways through space. Pilots, sailors, painters, sculptors and architects often have highly developed visual/spatial awareness and thinking. Musically speaking, this intelligence may present itself as the ability to choreograph movements (such as in a marching band or a Rhythmaze) or arrange items or people (as in a drum circle).

[2] From *National Standards for Arts Education*. Copyright © 1994 by Music Educators National Conference (MENC). Used by permission. The complete National Arts Standards and additional materials relating to the Standards are available from MENC: The National Association for Music Education, 1806 Robert Fulton Drive, Reston, VA 20191.

Kinesthetic/Bodily: The ability to use and manipulate objects, often with a great degree of physical skill, and to gain understanding through touch and movement. Athletes, dancers, surgeons and crafts people all have a highly developed kinesthetic intelligence. In music, this intelligence may surface as a natural technical ability on an instrument, or the ability to learn to play with little or no instruction. Drumming is a very physical art form. From the raising of hands and arms to the rhythmic swaying of the body, drumming offers a full body experience in making music.

Musical/Rhythmic: The ability to sense and identify differences and changes in pitch, timbre, tempo and rhythm. To feel and communicate ideas and emotions through sound and music. Composers, musicians, poets, sound therapists and instrument builders must all apply this intelligence to their craft. This intelligence is not contingent upon life experience or language, and as a result, is capable of being developed from a very early age. Musically, this ability is often evident in people who exhibit perfect pitch; those who make vocal "sound effects" when they describe something; remember melodies; identify people, animals or instruments based on their sound; recognize rhythms in words and phrases (as rappers & poets do); and have the ability to hear music in everyday sounds.

Interpersonal: The ability to interact with and effectively communicate with others. These people are often good listeners and are able to "read" people so as to gain insight into their thoughts and emotions. Teachers, social workers, therapists and actors are often people who relate well to others. An example of this intelligence may be reflected musically in a heightened sensitivity to the emotional qualities or 'message' of a piece of music or the ability to communicate meaning through music.

Intrapersonal: The ability to gain an accurate perception of oneself and use this information as a guiding factor in one's life. This kind of "reflective thinking" is evident in philosophers, theologians, psychologists and spiritual guides. This intelligence could be expressed in musical terms in an increased capacity to draw metaphors between musical and personal relationships (such as the steady pulse of a drum and one's own determination).

Naturalist: The ability to observe objects and events in nature and understand natural systems and patterns. This intelligence is evident in hunters, farmers, ecologists and meteorologists. Musically speaking, this intelligence could manifest itself through one's ability to draw parallels between natural rhythms and cycles and those found in musical works.

Music Therapy Applications (MT)

These are provided for the music therapist's convenience, but may be of use to the facilitator in health and wellness circles.

Preparation

These steps help create the setting for the activity. Note that preparation time is not included in the estimated **time span**.

Process

These are the steps of the core activity.

Extension

A variety of optional steps, variations, and alternatives are provided so that the facilitator can extend or modify an activity in a way that is appropriate for any specific group. These are suggestions only and can be modified or expanded upon depending on the needs and goals of the participants.

Discussion

The discussion segment is time for positive reflection that will reinforce connections and allow the participants to assimilate their experience in different ways. The length of the discussion segment will vary depending upon the type of event. In a classroom setting, the discussion will serve to reinforce and emphasize the focus elements of the activity, just as the discussion that takes place in a music therapy circle will reinforce the process that took place. A community circle discussion closes the event and so will tend to be brief. Team-building or training circles use the discussion time as a fundamental tool and may devote as much as half the total time of the event to it. Regardless of the length of the discussion, it is important to emphasize that there are no right or wrong answers. Encourage participants to speak in "I" statements to allow the experience to be seen from the angle of each individual, and remind them that every opinion is valid, even though they may not always agree.

Games and Activities

RAIN

This activity encourages students to use their imaginations and allows them to "play" with their instruments in a free-form setting. It's a great way to introduce basic musical concepts such as timbre and volume (without getting too technical), and it allows everyone to contribute in his or her own way.

Time span: 5–10 minutes

Instruments: body percussion and/or drums and small percussion

Focus: active participation, emulating sounds of nature, matching sounds with verbal cues, improvising, story telling

NS: 2 (performing), 3 (improvising), 4 (composing), 7 (evaluating), 8 (understanding relationships)

MI: verbal/linguistic, musical/rhythmic, naturalist

MT: reminiscence, reality orientation, attention span, impulse control, sensory stimulation, group leadership, self-esteem, creative self-expression, fine and gross motor skills, and abstract thinking

Preparation: Ask everyone in the group if they can remember the last time it rained. Ask them to describe what they noticed was happening before, during, and after the rain. Suggest they create their own "rain storm."

PROCESS

Describe the following scenario to the group. Invite them to play along, creating sounds that complement the action in the story (see examples in parentheses).

1. The wind starts to blow. *(rubbing hands together or rubbing the head of a drum)*
2. As the wind gets stronger, the leaves rattle and the wind whistles. *(tapping the side of a drum and whistling)*
3. Small drops of water start to fall from the sky. *(snapping fingers or finger tips on the drums)*
4. The droplets get bigger. *(light clapping, patting the thighs, or playing with hands on drums)*
5. Thunder comes! *(stomping feet, playing low tones on drums, or striking a gong)*
6. The storm passes through and gets lighter. *(reverse the process until the group is back to a gentle breeze)*
7. The sun comes out, and birds and other animal sounds are heard. *(students vocalize nature sounds)*

Extension

- Use percussion instruments instead of body percussion, such as playing shakers for wind, bells and triangles for soft rain, wood sounds for heavier rain, drums for loud rain and a gong for thunder.
- Try the sequence first using only body sounds, then do it again using instruments.
- Have students take turns narrating.
- Play the game with closed eyes.
- Segue from the storm to a rumble-roll, then into rhythm.
- Describe other scenes, like jungles, prairies, cities, planets, etc.

Discussion

- Did you notice a difference between having your eyes open and closed?
- Did it make you listen harder when you couldn't see the instruments being played?
- Did you see anyone creating sounds in ways that were new to you?
- What are some other musical sounds you hear when you're outside?
- How can you play other "nature" sounds on the instruments?

DRUM TALES

A great ice-breaker! Everyone loves a good story, and this game provides students with an opportunity to make up their own stories and share them with everyone else. Playing this game introduces students to the instruments in a gentle, informal way, allowing them to decide what their instrument is, where it came from, and what it's used for. Always different, always fun.

Note: This activity works best with small groups (up to 20 participants).

Time span: 1–3 minutes per student

Instruments: drums and percussion
Suggestions: Use a wide variety of standard and exotic percussion instruments. Caxixi, gankogui, maracas, guiro, talking drum, log drum, and other instruments that have unusual shapes may help spark the imagination.

Focus: active participation, creativity, composition, listening, public speaking

NS: 2 (performing), 3 (improvising), 4 (composing), 7 (evaluating), 8 (understanding relationships)

MI: interpersonal, verbal/linguistic

MT: creative self-expression, verbal communication, reality orientation, taking turns, peer awareness, and peer support

Preparation: Gather students in a circle. Distribute instruments, or have each student choose an instrument.

Process

1. Each student creates a story about his or her instrument. Encourage statements about the instrument's origin, how it traveled, who brought it and why, etc.

   Let students know they can use their imaginations and that it's OK to make up their story. Provide an example such as, "My instrument is a maraca and it came here on a boat from South America with lots of other maracas. They all grew there on a giant tree that made a big noise when the wind blew!"

2. Students take turns telling their stories, playing their instrument at the end.

   Tip: Remind students to talk about their own experiences and to be mindful of the time so everyone can have a turn. You might like to suggest they take only one minute each to share their stories.

Extension

- If your instrument was a tool, what would it be used for?
- If your instrument was an animal, what kind would it be?
- If your instrument was a house, who would live in it?
- What is the rhythm that is inside your instrument?
- Have everyone use the same instrument—see how many different things it can be.

Discussion

- What were some things about other people's stories you liked?
- Could you imagine that their story is real?

Note: I've presented this activity with children and adults. Both groups enjoy making up stories and using their imaginations to weave their instrument into a tale about someone's life or their own. With adult populations, I often find they use the opportunity to talk about themselves and past experiences. This process can prove to be very therapeutic as people share their stories with each other that often reflect issues of separation and reunion, friendship, family and love.

RUMBLE BALL

A real crowd-pleaser! This game works for all ages and involves the entire group in a way that makes it easy for everyone to participate. Students work with basic musical concepts such as timbre and volume, and associate musical ideas with movement. Good for visual learners. Drumming has never been so playful!

Time span: 5–10 minutes

Instruments: hand percussion, drums
Suggestions: Use members from all four timbre groups (drums, wood, shakers, metal).

Other materials: a small rubber ball

Focus: improvisation, matching sound with movement, performing on instruments, active participation, leadership, spatial awareness

NS: 2 (performing), 3 (improvising), 4 (composing), 5 (reading), 7 (evaluating)

MI: visual/spatial, musical/rhythmic, kinesthetic/bodily

MT: creativity, group teamwork, leadership skills, motor skills (playing and using the ball), social interactions, taking turns, attention span, and self-esteem

Preparation: Form a large circle. Provide students with a variety of drums and percussion instruments.

Process

1. Upon entering the circle, play with the ball for a couple of minutes without giving instructions to the students. Establish three modes of play: **bouncing, rolling,** and **tossing.**

2. Ask students to provide adjectives that best describe the action of the ball bouncing on the floor. **Example:** sudden, hard, low, etc. *Tip: When working with children, ask for a volunteer to define the word "adjective" for the group.*

3. Ask students which instruments or instrument groups are best described by the adjectives they provided.
   Example: The drums and wood instruments sound *hard* and *low*, therefore, they work well as the bouncing sounds.

4. Invite students with the appropriate instruments to play along with the specific action. "Let's hear everyone with drums and wood sounds play when the ball bounces on the floor." Take a minute to practice with that group.

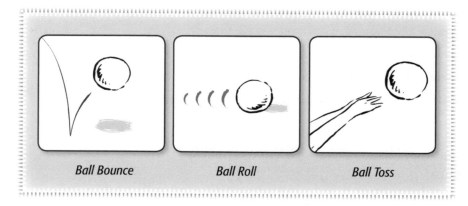

Ball Bounce   *Ball Roll*   *Ball Toss*

5. Repeat step 2–4 for the actions **rolling** (sustained sounds—shakers, etc.) and **tossing** (high sounds—bells, tambourines, etc).

6. Play with the ball using all three modes, and have students match the movements.

7. Add another student to share the ball with you, and then substitute another student for yourself. Change leaders often to give everyone an opportunity to lead (the new leader swaps instruments with the previous leader).

Extension

- Ask students if they can think of other actions to link up with the sounds, such as holding still, spinning on the floor, balancing it on one's head, etc.
- Substitute body percussion or vocals for instruments.
- Use balls of different colors to cue different arcs (sections of the circle) or instrument groups.
- Use Orff instruments grouped by pitch or instrument type.
- Use an "invisible" ball.

Discussion

- What did you like about this activity?
- Did you see a leader create a new action? How did you respond?
- What are some other actions we could match with sound?
- Do we need a ball to do this activity?

FOLEY

Ever wanted to make sound effects for theatre or the movies? Now you can. Students take turns creating their own "sound track" for various activities. This game encourages creative thinking, helps associate movement with music, and helps to develop gross and fine motor skills. It's musical theatre—drummer style.

Time span: 20–30 minutes

Instruments: hand percussion, drums
Suggestions: Provide instruments with a variety of qualities (hard and soft, high and low, etc.) such as low drums, woodblocks, tambourines, shakers, triangles.

Focus: matching sound with movement, observing environmental rhythms, improvising, leadership, spatial awareness

NS: 2 (performing), 3 (improvising), 4 (composing), 7 (evaluating), 8 (understanding relationships)

MI: visual/spatial, musical/rhythmic, bodily/kinesthetic, interpersonal, naturalist

MT: leadership skills, non-verbal communication, self-esteem, reality orientation, attention span, impulse control, abstract thinking, social interactions and teamwork

Preparation: Explain that a *foley artist* is someone who makes sound effects for movies and adds noises like footsteps, doors opening and closing, and even eating sounds to films. In this activity, everyone becomes a foley artist by making sounds to match the "actors'" movements.

Process

1. Ask a volunteer you've chosen from the circle to mimic a recognizable activity such as playing a sport or doing work around the house.

    Tip: It may be helpful to demonstrate a few actions yourself, inviting everyone to join you, before choosing an individual.

2. Ask students to analyze what the actor is doing and to create sound effects with their instruments to match and emphasize the actions.
    Example: The actor is digging a hole and dumping the dirt nearby. The group decides that the drums will play together when the shovel hits the ground. The wood sounds will play when he walks across the ground, and the shakers, bells, and triangles play when the dirt is thrown into a pile.

    Tip: If the group is having trouble deciding which sounds to use, choose someone to be the "director." They get to decide which sounds best represent aspects of the motion. Encourage the director to include all the sounds of the circle so no one is left out.

3. Add more actors to make complementary movements and have the foley artists match their movements with different sounds. You may decide to have different sections of the circle or instrument groups play for different actors.
    Example: The drums play for an actor who is digging a hole, while the woodblocks play for an actor who is hammering nails.

4. Rotate participants through the different roles. You may wish to rotate instruments so that everyone gets a turn playing each type of instrument.

Extension

- Perform using only vocal sounds or body percussion.
- Ask students to make sounds that **don't** match the action.
- Break into smaller groups, and have each group perform their "scene."
- Have each group choose a general topic for their scene (sports, construction, games, cooking, etc.).

Discussion

- Was it easy to figure out what the activities were supposed to be?
- Did the sounds match the actions well? Why or why not?
- What made it easy or difficult to follow the action?

RHYTHMAZE

Put on your thinking caps! This activity involves art and geometry skills while developing team work and creativity. It's a social event where everyone can participate and contribute. Visual learners will feel at home as they "draw" out their ideas and share them with the group.

Time span: 20–30 minutes

Instruments: small drums and percussion
Suggestions: Shakers, finger cymbals, woodblocks, frog raspers, small frame drums, maracas, agogo, triangles.

Other materials: masking tape

Tip: Painter's tape is less sticky and easier to remove than regular tape.

Focus: active participation, concentration, spatial awareness, geometric concepts, composing & arranging music, teamwork, awareness of self and others, cross curriculum (drawing, design)

NS: 2 (performing), 3 (improvising), 6 (listening), 7 (evaluating), 8 (understanding relationships)

MI: visual/spatial, logical/mathematical, kinesthetic/bodily, interpersonal

MT: leadership skills, modeling behaviors, creativity, teamwork, cognitive skills, motor skills (fine and gross), attention span, reality orientation, impulse control

Preparation: Explain the concept of a *Rhythmaze*. Designed with lines that do not cross, it provides a path for the group to travel that begins at the edge of the circle, travels to the center, and goes back out to the edge again.

Note: A Rhythmaze is not the same as a labyrinth. In a Rhythmaze, the path starts at the edge, works its way to the center, then continues until it reaches the edge again. In a labyrinth, the path starts at the edge and ends at the center, so the same path is used to return to the edge.

Have all the students design and draw their individual version of a Rhythmaze on a piece of paper. Invite them to form a large circle (use chairs or tape to designate the boundary if needed).

Tip: For younger students, use tape to create a Rhythmaze on the floor. This makes it easier to follow.

Some Rhythmaze examples:

Process

1. Before handing out instruments, choose someone to lead the group through his or her Rhythmaze from the edge, to the center, and back out to the edge.

2. Distribute hand-held instruments.

3. Have everyone step to a steady beat (walking tempo) and play their instruments to the beat.

4. While everyone is playing, have the leader walk the Rhythmaze path to the center and back to the edge while the group follows. The goal is to move from the outside of the circle, through the center, and back. Suggest that everyone notices how the "mix" (the relative volumes of the instruments) changes as they are walking the Rhythmaze.

5. If the group ends up back in a circle, great! If not, process the outcome with the group and try

it again. Rotate leaders so all participants get a chance to walk their Rhythmaze path with the group. You may take this opportunity to remind the new leader that he or she may choose a faster or slower tempo than the previous leader but to be sure to choose a tempo that will help the group succeed.

Extension

- Half the group plays instruments while the other half walks the Rhythmaze.
- Participants follow all the leader's cues as they walk. Perhaps they will choose certain portions of the path where they will play softly or walk in a different way (arms up/down, walking sideways, big/little steps, etc.).

Discussion

- How did you feel when you were in the middle of the Rhythmaze with everyone else around you?
- Did the music change as you walked along the path?
- How did you visualize your maze when it was your turn to lead?
- What advice would you give someone who wanted to design a Rhythmaze?

DRUM CALL

This simple game helps groups get into the groove and develop their listening skills as they follow cues from the facilitator. It works with small to large groups and may be scaled to various levels of complexity. It helps develop reflexes, math skills and creativity. Get ready—the drum is calling!

Time span: 5–10 minutes

Instruments: drums and percussion; voice or body percussion
Suggestions: Instruments with a fast decay such as wood sounds, drums, cowbells, etc.

Focus: active participation, taking turns, composition, leadership, awareness of self and others

NS: 2 (performing), 3 (improvising), 4 (composing), 7 (evaluating), 8 (understanding relationships)

MI: verbal/linguistic, musical/rhythmic, mathematical/logical, interpersonal

MT: creative self-expression, verbal communication, taking turns, peer awareness, peer support

Preparation: Gather students in a circle. Distribute instruments or have each student choose an instrument

Process

1. Explain that when you call out "one," everyone is to play one note (a quarter note, *Ta*) on their instrument. When you call out "two," everyone plays two notes (eighth notes, *Ti–Ti*).
2. Call out numbers ("one" and "two") in rhythm while the group responds.
3. Rotate leadership around the circle so everyone gets a turn calling out different numbers for the group.

Extension

Variation: Got Rap?

I like to introduce this activity in rap-style.

1. Call out an instruction in rhythm: "When I say [call], you say [response]."
2. Say the call and have the group respond. (Repeat)

   Example: *(F = Facilitator   G = Group)*

   F: " When I say *Ha,* you say *Ho.*"

   F: "Ha" G: "Ho"

   F: "Ha" G: "Ho"

Tip: It may help to double-up the instruction and call & response phrases (2 and 4 times, respectively).

3. Try creating and combining 2-beat phrases to form a group chant.

Examples:

   F: "Playing"   G: "drums"

   F: "So much"   G: "fun"

   F: "Feel the"   G: "rhythm"

   F: "Every"   G: "one"

Tip: Don't forget to ask your students for their ideas and suggestions!

Variation: Got Math?

Call out a simple math question and have the students play the answer on their instruments.

Examples: *(F = Facilitator G = Group)*

F: "Five minus three is"   *G:* BOOM (rest), BAM (rest)

F: "Two plus two is"   *G:* BOOM, BAM, BIFF, BONG

F: "Three plus two is"   *G:* BOOM, BAM, PLING–PLANG, PLONG

F: "Twelve minus five is"   *G:* BOOM–BAM, BIFF–BING, PLING–PLANG, PLONG

Other Variations

- Use only hand signals to cue the group.
- Use different languages such as Spanish ("uno," "dos"), French ("un," "deux"), Chinese ("ee," "er"), etc.
- Add the numbers "four" (sixteenth notes), "three" (triplet or two sixteenths and one eighth note), and "zero" (rest) to make it more challenging.
- Experiment with different tempos and dynamics.

- Call out the name of something that represents a specific number, such as "wheels on a bicycle" for two, "pints in a gallon" for four, "corners on a triangle" for three. This activity promotes quick thinking and response, and can help students learn new information at the same time. You may wish to choose a theme or topic such as animals (number of legs or ?), or units of measurement (pints in a gallon, feet in a yard, etc.).

- Call out a specific type of note such as "quarter note," "eighth notes," or "whole note." Have students fill the space with those notes.

- Have the group respond with the "opposite" of what is called out (for example, "high" for "low," "two" for "one," etc.).

  Tip: For groups of young or inexperienced students, try having everyone play notes of the same value for each group of 1, 2, 3, or 4 notes.

Discussion

- What was challenging?

- Did someone give an unexpected cue when it was their turn? How did you respond?

- What are some other ways someone could cue the group?

SECRET SONG

Can you keep a secret? Not if the group can guess your song! Participants take turns sharing their favorite rhymes as the group tries to guess which song they're playing and joins in. It's like musical charades!

Time span: 10–15 minutes

Instruments: drums and percussion; voice or body percussion
Suggestions: Small, hand-held instruments may help facilitate movement activities.

Focus: active participation, taking turns, leadership, listening, sharing

NS: 2 (performing), 3 (improvising), 4 (composing), 7 (evaluating)

MI: verbal/linguistic, musical/rhythmic, interpersonal

MT: creative self-expression, verbal communication, taking turns, peer awareness, peer support

Preparation: Gather students in a circle. Distribute instruments or have each student choose an instrument.

Process

1. Play the rhythm of a common or popular song on your instrument (or use body percussion). Ask the group to guess which song it's from and play along. (Note: Choose an easy song such as "Row, Row, Row Your Boat" or "Twinkle, Twinkle, Little Star.") Repeat the rhythm if no one guesses it the first time through.

2. If students still can't guess which song it is after two times through, play it again while you sing along. Invite everyone to sing and play along with you as you finish the song.

3. Ask for volunteers to choose and play a rhythm of another song, inviting everyone to play along if they think they know which song it is.

4. Rotate turns around the circle to give everyone a chance to present a secret song.

Extension

- Have students create movements or dances that reflect the rhythm or theme of the song.

- Have students alternate between different body percussion sounds, instruments and/or movements. For example: Clap the song, step the song, play the song, sing the song.

- Divide the group into equal sections and perform the above sequence in canon (starting at equal intervals).

Discussion

- Were there any songs with the same rhythm? If not, can you think of any?

- Did someone give an unexpected cue when it was their turn? How did you respond?

- What are some other ways we could represent the song?

ORBIT

Round and round, the rhythm goes, where it stops, nobody knows! Rhythms and smiles travel in circles as participants develop important skills like listening, sharing and responding to cues. This is a wonderful activity to develop awareness of others, and timing!

Time span: 20–30 minutes

Instruments: body percussion, voice and/or drums and percussion
Suggestions: A variety of distinct sounds works best. Separate similar instruments.

Focus: active listening, teamwork, imagination, creativity, awareness of self and others, cross-curriculum studies (solar system/ atoms, anything else that orbits or has an orbiting body could be related)

NS: 2 (performing), 3 (improvising), 4 (composing), 7 (evaluating), 8 (understanding relationships)

MI: musical/rhythmic, interpersonal, mathematical/logical

MT: non-verbal communication, reality orientation, attention span, creative self expression, impulse control, following directions, motor-skill development

Preparation: Gather in a circle with drums and/or small hand percussion.

Process

1. Let the group know the object of this activity is to have a sound or rhythmic phrase travel around the circle in an orbit (as in the popular game "telephone").
2. Orbit a rhythmic phrase around the circle by having each student take a turn playing four, evenly spaced notes (*Ti–Ti–Ti–Ti*).
3. Ask them to see if they can keep the space between the notes the same from one person to the next (so as to keep a steady rhythm).
4. Try orbiting three- and two-note phrases. See how fast the group can play and still keep the rhythm steady.

Music Therapy Note: For a simple application, the facilitator could point (cue) each person with one beat. The facilitator determines the tempo, helps the participants focus on the group leader, and keeps the sound orbiting around the circle.

Extension

- Try this exercise with eyes closed and at different tempos.
- Orbit different rhythmic combinations such as these:

1	+	2	+	3	+	4	+
•		•		•	•	•	
•	•		•	•		•	
•	•	•	•	•			
•			•	•	•	•	

- Create a cue that will bounce the orbiting sound in the other direction such as "boing!" Make an agreement that each student may "bounce" the orbit whenever they want (but only once).
- Have students randomly choose the next player with a visual cue by playing to another student. **Example:** Student looks at someone else while still playing to indicate he or she will be the next one to play.
- Orbit two sounds in opposite directions. Watch what happens when they reach one person and try to cross paths!

- Have one student play an improvised phrase (two or four beats long). Have the next student echo the first student's phrase and add a different phrase of equal length. Have the next student echo the second student's phrase and add a different phrase of their own.

Example:

1. Student 1 plays phrase A.

2. Student 2 echoes phrase A and adds B (AB).

3. Student 3 echoes phrase B and adds C (BC).

4. Continue around the circle.

Tip: Before trying this game with instruments, practice this concept with the group by having each student say letters of the alphabet. **Example:** *A, AB, BC, CD, DE, etc.*

- Try physically orbiting certain instruments around the circle such as shakers, rattles, rain sticks (small, lightweight instruments that don't require beaters work best). Explain that the object is not to let the sound stop while passing the instruments from person to person. **Example:** Students keep a rattle shaking as they pass it, or rotate a rain stick so the sound from the instrument is continuous from one person to the next.

Note: This exercise allows participants to work together to keep the sound constant, and it encourages sharing and gives everyone an opportunity to play a wide variety of instruments. It's also a lot of fun!

Orbit Multiple

- Introduce patterns more frequently so there are two, three, or even four of them orbiting the circle at the same time. Be sure to point out that students need to listen to the person next to them for their cue and not be thrown off by what others are doing across the circle.

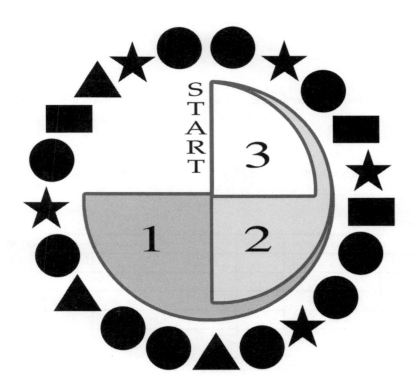

Discussion

- What changed for you when you closed your eyes?
- What happened when two orbits overlapped?
- Where did you focus your attention?
- If the orbiting rhythm was "lost in space," what could have helped prevent that from happening?
- How is playing this game like having a conversation?

HAVE A BALL

This can be used as an ice-breaker or to help students move gently into the rhythmic setting as they learn about everyone in the circle. Sharing, awareness of self and others, and motor skills are developed in a friendly atmosphere. Great for groups who are meeting for the first time!

Time span: 5–10 Minutes

Instruments: small percussion (soft sounds such as small shakers or rattles), body percussion
Suggestions: Shakers, small hand drums, finger cymbals, scrapers, frog raspers, Boomwhaker percussion tubes and most low-volume instruments.

Other materials: rubber or foam ball, or ball of yarn

Focus: sharing, cooperation, keeping a steady beat, listening, learning about peers

NS: 2 (performing), 3 (improvising), 4 (composing), 7 (evaluating)

MI: musical/rhythmic, interpersonal, visual/spatial, verbal/linguistic

MT: verbal and non-verbal communication skills, attention span, gross and fine motor skills (passing and playing), self-esteem, reality orientation, acknowledging others in the group

Preparation: Sit in a circle, preferably on the floor. Have a small rubber or foam ball (or one made of yarn) ready to pass between participants. Place a small percussion instrument in front of each participant. Ask everyone to leave their instruments on the floor until they get the ball.

Process

1. Begin by holding the ball.
2. Have everyone pat their thighs to a steady beat.
3. Speaking in rhythm, state your name and share something about yourself. **Example:** "My name is Robert and I like to draw" (align strong syllables with strong beats when possible.)
4. Roll the ball to someone across the circle and pick up your instrument and play along with the beat.
5. The student who gets the ball introduces himself (in rhythm).
6. The student then rolls the ball to someone else (who is still patting their thighs) and picks up their instrument, playing along with the beat.
7. The game continues until everyone has been introduced and is playing an instrument.

   Note: As more members of the group move from patting to playing, the volume level will increase. Ask or motion for everyone to play softly when someone is speaking. This will help everyone develop their listening skills, sense of dynamics and sensitivity as they learn to share the sonic space.

Extension

- Once everyone has been introduced, reverse the game and return to patting.
- Reverse game alternative: See if the student who *catches* the ball can tell the group about the person who rolled it (remember to always speak in rhythm).

- Use a ball of yarn or string that unravels as it is rolled from person to person. Each person who catches the ball will have to secure the string when they roll it, either by holding it in their hand at ground level, or by placing it under their foot or leg. The result is a connective "web" that can then be held between everyone in the group. Raise the web high in the air for a dramatic metaphor of connection and beauty.

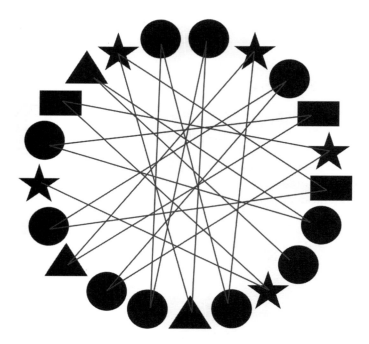

Discussion

- Did you learn something new about your peers?
- Did you play differently when someone was talking?
- If creating the "web," what does this web represent?
- Is it possible to feel this connection without the string? How?
- What are some other "webs" that connect us?

LET'S ALL PLAY OUR DRUM!

This game always keeps students on the edge of their seats, listening carefully, and ready to PLAY! It's perfect as an interlude to an ongoing jam session or as an elimination game. Students benefit greatly from taking the leader position where they will be challenged to make full use of their rhythmic skills.

Time span: 10–15 minutes

Instruments: drums, percussion and/or body percussion
Suggestions: Provide a variety of instruments from all four timbre groups (drums, wood, shakers, metal).

Focus: active listening, responding to cues, rhythm and tempo awareness

NS: 2 (performing), 3 (improvising), 4 (composing), 6 (listening), 7 (evaluating)

MI: verbal/linguistic, musical/rhythmic, mathematical/logical

MT: creativity, leadership, self-esteem, short-term memory development, sequencing, modeling behaviors, communication, social interaction, reality orientation, sound discrimination, attention span, impulse control, taking turns, motor skills

Preparation: Have everyone form a circle (standing or sitting). Provide an assortment of drums and percussion instruments.

Process

1. Ask everyone to stand, leaving the instruments for the moment.

2. Have the group match your actions for the capitalized words (one note only) as you introduce and combine the following cues:

   "Let's all *clap* our HANDS"

   "Let's all *snap* our FINGERS"

   "Let's all *pat* our THIGHS"

   "Let's all *stomp* our FEET"

   Note: Use the rhythm Ti–Ti–Ti–Ti–Toe for the above examples. Present one example several times through before adding the next.

3. Ask students to suggest other actions:

   "Let's all __?__ our __?__"

   Add the students' ideas to the first four and continue, changing the tempo and subject of the cues.

4. Orbit the leadership role around the circle, inviting students to provide new actions.

5. Move to the instruments and present phrases that cue specific groups of instruments:

   "Let's all *ring* our BELLS"

   "Let's all *clack* our BLOCKS"

   "Let's all *shake* our RATTLES"

   "Let's all *play* our DRUMS"

6. Continue the game with the new cues, pausing occasionally to ask the participants if they can suggest other possible combinations.

Extension

Variation 1

1. Let everyone know that when you say, "Let's all play our DRUM," that everyone is to play their instrument on "DRUM" (one hit), no matter which kind of instrument they have.

2. Say the cue phrase at different tempos and volumes.

3. Shorten the verbal cue to "All play our DRUM" and "Play our DRUM."

4. Transfer the cue to an instrument by playing the phrase as you say it, then only playing it. Continue playing the game, while varying the tempo and dynamics of the cue.

Variation 2

1. Introduce a longer phrase and play only on the last note (the word "FUN" in the following example).

1	+	2	+	3	+	4	+	1	+	2	+	3	+	4	+
Let's	all	play	our	drum	be-	cause	it's	so		much		FUN.			

2. Take away some of the last words (notes) so participants have to feel the beat through a rest before they play. This becomes more challenging as the cue becomes shorter.

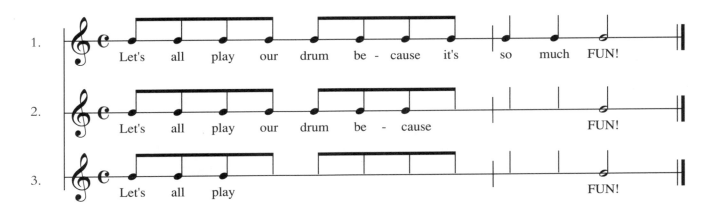

3. Ask everyone to try this with their eyes closed.

4. Vary the tempo to make this more challenging.

Discussion

- Did anyone suggest a movement that you particularly liked?
- What made the cues easy or difficult to follow?
- What advice would you give to someone who was about to try this?
- What are some other phrases we could use as a cue?

SOUND MACHINE

Get up and get moving! This activity is like a mini-workout that will bring out the crazy, creative energy of any group. Students work together to create their own inter-dependant machines that illustrate the importance of timing, teamwork and flexibility.

Time span: 20–30 minutes

Instruments: hand percussion or frame drums with mallets
Suggestions: Rainbow hand drums played with mallets, Boomwhacker percussion tubes, individual Joia tubes, any instruments that are played with sticks or mallets.

Focus: communication, collaboration, keeping a steady beat, moving in rhythm, teamwork, spatial awareness of self and others

NS: 2 (performing), 3 (improvising), 4 (composing), 6 (listening), 7 (evaluating)

MI: musical/rhythmic, bodily/kinesthetic, visual/spatial, interpersonal

MT: fine and gross motor skills, teamwork, modeling behaviors, attention span, self-esteem, social communication/interaction, impulse control, relationship development

Preparation: Choose instruments that can be played while moving around. If possible, provide hand drums and mallets of at least two different colors.

Process

1. Ask the group for examples of objects that have a lot of parts that move together in rhythm (watches, a factory, a motor, etc). Discuss the concept of synchronization and interdependency.

2. Play or clap a simple rhythm and ask everyone to imagine they are part of a big machine, and to make a movement that is in sync with the pulse (movements may include reaching, lifting, stepping, bending, etc.). Provide them with some ideas by demonstrating large movements through space.

3. Ask students to choose a partner and make complementary movements that utilize some of the same space (for example, if one stops the other would have to stop or they might bump into each other). Remind them that they have legs! (most students tend to focus on their arms only). Working in phrases of eight beats is preferred.

Tip: Suggest they start by choosing one person to establish a movement, then have the other add a complementary movement. Reverse the roles and repeat so everyone experiences both perspectives.

4. Play a steady beat while the groups work together.

5. Repeat above, inviting students to play small percussion instruments or hand drums while moving together. They can play their own, each other's, or a combination.

Extension

• Create groups of three or four students (or combine two groups of two and see if their movements can work together).

• Group students by instrument or mallet color.

Variation: Making the BIG Machine

1. Invite one student to go to the center of the circle and play a rhythm that involves reaching, stepping, bending, etc., on his or her instrument.

2. Invite or choose another student to join the first one, playing a part that fits musically with the first and that moves in a way that connects with them (utilizing some of the same space, but not physically touching).

3. Invite or choose others to join the group, one at a time, until everyone is participating. As people join the group they'll find unique ways of fitting in, both in music and movement. The result is a giant "sound machine" that is moving in rhythm!

Alternatives

- As people join in, have them play someone else's instrument and make theirs available for the next person who joins in (frame drums played with mallets work well).

- Cue tempo changes: Speed up until the "machine" breaks apart, or slow down until it "runs out of fuel."

- Suggest group motion: Can the Machine move around? Have some people create a "machine," then invite others to move through it.

Discussion

- Was it important for everyone to work together? Why?

- Which kinds of movements worked best?

- Were some groups playing longer or shorter phrases than your group?

- How did changing the tempo affect the group's movements and music?

- What advice would you give to a person or group who wanted to try this?

PIECES OF EIGHT

This is a wonderful game that shows students the principle of synergy—when the result is greater than the sum of their individual effects. It's also a great way to illustrate the beauty of simplicity, diversity and working together to create music that is unique and always "in the moment."

Time span: 10–15 minutes

Instruments: drums and percussion

    Suggestions: A variety of hand drums, wood sounds, shakers and metal; Boomwhacker percussion tubes or separate Joia tubes.

    Focus: active participation, concentration, composing and arranging music, teamwork, listening, diversity appreciation, math concepts

    NS: 2 (performing), 3 (improvising), 4 (composing), 6 (listening), 7 (evaluating)

    MI: logical/mathematical, rhythmic/musical, interpersonal

    MT: cognitive skills, sequencing, reality orientation, motor skills, impulse control, self-esteem, taking turns, following directions, attention span

    Preparation: Gather students in a circle, Distribute instruments.

Process

1. Ask students to silently choose a number from 1 to 8. Explain that you will be counting out loud from 1 to 8 in rhythm (repeating).

2. Ask students to play one note on their instrument each time you reach their number.

3. Clap in rhythm and count for the group. (You can stop counting out loud once the students are playing on their own.) Invite everyone to listen to the drum melody that results.

4. Suggest they try to find the people who are playing on the same beat as they are.

5. After a couple of minutes, suggest that everyone adds one note (playing 2 notes per each 8-beat phrase).

6. If desired, add more notes over time.

7. When it feels appropriate, reduce the number of notes by one until everyone is back to playing 1 note per 8 beats.

8. Bring the activity to a close by saying "Last time through," or cue a fade out.

1	2	3	4	5	6	7	8
	█						
					█		
							█
						█	
			█				
					█		
		█					
█							
						█	
			█				
				█			
█							

The music is full, even when everyone only plays one note!

Extension

- Group the circle into arcs, featuring one arc at a time while the others rest and listen. Rotate through the arcs in even phrases (four or eight phrases of 8 beats, for example). Reduce the number of phrases so the playing orbits more quickly around the circle.

- Create two phrases of 8 beats each and have participants play on different numbers in each 8-beat phrase or play only one note for both phrases (1 note per 16 beats).

- Increase or decrease the tempo and/or volume.

- Have everyone play on the beats of their birthday. **Example:** 25th plays on 2 and 5, 14th plays on 1 and 4, 6th plays on 6, 29th plays on 2 and ?

- If playing hand-held percussion, have participants move and form groups of those playing the same beats. Have them choose a different beat and form new groups.

- Have everyone play a different sound when a certain cue is given such as brushing the head of a drum with the fingers, tapping the drum's edge, or playing the instrument of the person to the right.

- Try this as a movement exercise where all the members take a step (or play a body percussion sound) on their number(s).

Discussion

- What was challenging about this activity?

- Was there something you did that made it easier?

- Did you notice anyone doing something that you especially liked?

- Did everyone need to play a lot of notes for the music to sound full?

- Did the music remind you of anything?

- What would this look like in a drawing?

RHYTHMASIZE YOUR NAME

What's in a name? Let's find out! This activity helps students develop musical ideas from a single source. It's a great way to create multi-layered parts that are interrelated, and illustrates musical concepts such as accents, phrasing and variation. It's also a nice way to honor a particular student or special occasion.

Time span: 5–10 minutes

Instruments: voice and percussion
> *Suggestions:* *A variety from the four timbre groups (drums, wood, shakers, metal).*

> **Focus:** Learning names, developing music from speech, learning about accents and speech inflection, developing many ideas from one source, appreciation of diversity

> **NS:** 2 (performing), 3 (improvising), 4 (composing), 6 (listening), 7 (evaluating)

> **MI:** verbal/linguistic, musical/rhythmic, interpersonal

> **MT:** cognitive skills, acknowledgement of peers, attention span, self-esteem, verbal communication, leadership skills, reality orientation

> **Preparation**: Gather with instruments in a circle. Choose someone's name (first name, last initial, nick-name, etc.) to use as source material for the activity.

Process

1. Have the person you chose state his name in rhythm as he claps his hands (or plays his drum) on the accented syllables.

> **Example:** *Name* BRI-an JA-cob-son   *Rhythm* TA ta TI-ti ta

2. Invite everyone to say that person's name with you in rhythm four times.

3. Ask the group to create three or four examples of how this name might be said in different ways. For example, whispering (as if in class), calling out loud (as if from a distance), scolding (as if the person is in trouble!), quickly (as if surprised to see them), etc. Repeat the previous step for each example.

4. Ask the group if they think all the ways in which to say that person's name have the same rhythm. Did the accents change? Did the tempo stay the same or did it get slower or faster?

5. Group participants into sections and explore ways to chant the various versions of the name together in rhythm.

6. Have students first transfer their chant to body percussion, then to the instruments.

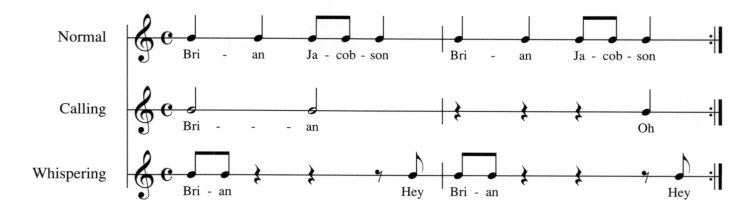

Extension

- Play as above but have them select instruments that match the sound quality of the words (sustaining sounds for longer syllables, soft sounds for whispering, etc.).

- Create an arrangement by chanting each version of the name four times. Have different sections of the group chant it in canon (starting at regular intervals). Expand your arrangement by alternating between chanting, body percussion and playing the instruments.
- Play the game with other student's names, different kinds of words (animals, states/capitols, presidents, etc.), or even short phrases (what you had for breakfast, how you got to school, etc.)

Discussion

- Were some names easier to work with than others? Why?
- Did the tempo of the name change as the group's vocal inflection changed? Why?
- Why do we accent certain parts of words?
- Why do we accent certain parts of music?
- Does it affect our ability to communicate when e-VER-y syl-LA-ble is ac-cen-TED dif-FER-ent-ly than we are used to?
- How does it change the feel of the music when we change the accents?
- Why do people who speak other languages have different accents when they speak our language?
- Do you like to listen to other people's accents? Why?

SIGNALS: HANDS

Students create their own team-based notation in this fast-moving activity. This "get out of your seat and move to the beat" game involves creativity, social skills, visual cues and timing. It's also a great way to develop leadership skills, non-verbal communication, gross motor skills and teamwork—and the leaders get an arm workout!

Time span: 10–15 minutes

Instruments: drums & percussion, or body percussion
Suggestions: Try this with a variety or all the same type of instruments. For faster tempos, use instruments that can be played with both hands such as hand drums or temple blocks with two mallets.

Focus: associating sound with movement, creating and notating music, following non-verbal cues, teamwork, math concepts, spatial awareness, awareness of self and others

NS: 2 (performing), 3 (improvising), 4 (composing), 5 (notating), 6 (listening), 7 (evaluating)

MI: visual/spatial, musical/rhythmic, mathematical/logical, kinesthetic/bodily, interpersonal

MT: motor-skill development, leadership skills, self esteem, social interactions, attention span, reality orientation

Preparation: Form a large circle. Provide instruments.

Process

1. Step in rhythm and have students simply feel the beat without playing (pat your chest to show "feeling" the beat).
2. While continuing to step in rhythm, hold up one hand to signal playing one-note-per-beat (1/4 note) and invite students to play their instruments or clap along (accent the beat with your hand).
3. Hold up two hands to signal two-notes-per-beat (1/8th notes).
4. Lower hands to signal resting (still feeling the pulse).
5. Experiment with these three modes of play (1–2 minutes) then ask for a volunteer(s) to lead the group.
6. Add another student to follow the leader to create a 2-beat phrase (the leader is beat 1 and the follower is beat 2).

   Tip: Ask the leaders to make hand gestures to accent the notes of their beat as the group plays along. You may wish to pause and have a brief discussion with the group as to what would make it easier to follow the leaders.

   Examples:

   • Leaders will hold their position for at least four cycles to give the group a chance to adjust to the new rhythm.

   • Leaders will make clear movements, only changing *after* the beat and not *on* it.

Music Therapy Note: This might prove to be a challenging activity for therapeutic applications. For best results, try a simplified version or only attempt this with high-functioning groups. The next game, Signals: Feet, may be a better choice as it provides a visual framework upon which to build.

Extension

• Have half the circle follow one person or group, and the other half follow another person or group.

• Add more leaders to create even longer rhythmic phrases (3, 4, 6, or 8 beats).

one note   two notes   rest

- Design different signals for rhythms and dynamics (shaking hands for a roll, hand shapes to indicate techniques such as scraping, fingers only, staccato (short sounds), legato (long sounds)
- Transfer the rhythm(s) of the group to standard or iconic notation.
- Designate the leader's right hand as the downbeat and the left as the upbeats.
- If changing signals on-the-fly is difficult, try having the leaders form a new pattern during a 4-beat break (rest), then have the group play the new pattern four times through. Start a new pattern with the 4-beat break each time to allow the leaders time to change their signals.

1–2–3–4	1–2–3–4	1–2–3–4	1–2–3–4
Play	Play	Play	Change

Discussion

- What was challenging about this activity?
- What advice would you give to someone who was about to try this?
- Is there another name for what the leaders were providing? (Hint: *Notation*)
- What are some other ways music can be "notated"? (Hint: artwork, clothing, structures, etc.)
- What would make it easier to do the next time?
- Can you think of some other ways the leaders could signal musical elements?

SIGNALS: FEET

We're not dancing—we're drumming with our feet! This activity helps get students moving and presents many opportunities for teamwork and creativity. Students are challenged to work together to create in-the-moment notation that requires lots of listening, self-awareness and awareness of others.

Time span: 15–20 minutes

Instruments: drums and percussion, or body percussion
Suggestions: Try this with a variety or all the same type of instruments. For faster tempos, use instruments that can be played with both hands such as hand drums or temple blocks with two mallets.

Other materials: Four hoops, or masking-tape squares.

Focus: associating sound with movement, creating and notating music, following non-verbal cues, teamwork, math concepts, awareness of self and others

NS: 2 (performing), 3 (improvising), 4 (composing), 5, (notating), 6 (listening), 7 (evaluating)

MI: visual/spatial, musical/rhythmic, mathematical/logical, kinesthetic/bodily, interpersonal

MT: motor skills, non-verbal communication, teamwork, leadership skills, self-esteem, impulse control, attention span, taking turns, reality orientation

Preparation: Place the four hoops in a straight line on the floor. Form a circle around the hoops and provide participants with instruments.

Process

1. Ask for four volunteers to be the leaders.
2. Have one student stand in each of the four hoops.
3. Explain that a leader can be in one of three positions: inside the hoop with feet together (group plays one note per beat), inside the hoop with feet spread apart (group plays two notes per beat), or outside the hoop (group rests).

   Tip: You may wish to start by modeling these three modes yourself, as in the game Signals: Hands.

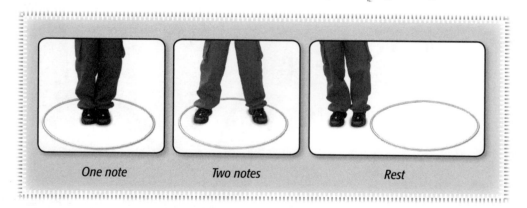

| One note | Two notes | Rest |

4. Designate each hoop as one beat of a 4-beat phrase. It may help to have one hoop that is a different color to use as beat 1.

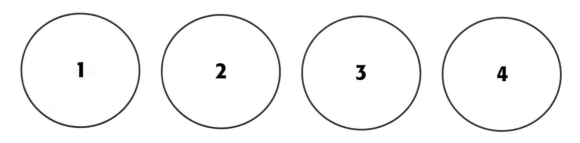

5. Ask students to follow the signals from the four leaders, playing once per beat when their feet are together, twice when their feet are apart and resting when they are not in their hoop.

6. Play a steady beat on a cowbell or rattle to help keep the group playing together. You may need to count out loud if some students lose track of the phrase. Change leaders often to give everyone a turn.

Tip: It may help to have some general rules for the leaders, such as the following:

• A leader's foot position must be clear.

• A leader should try to give the group as much time as possible to adjust to the new position by moving right after their beat and not just before.

• A leader can help the group adjust to the new pattern by holding the same position for at least four cycles.

• A leader can help the group by making a subtle movement on his or her beat, such as bending the knees or nodding the head.

Extension

• Keep the hoops and leaders in the same position, but reverse the direction in which the beats are read.

• Divide the group in two and have them read the rhythms in opposite directions.

• Add or remove hoops to create phrases of different lengths.

• Transfer the rhythm(s) of the group to standard or iconic notation.

• Ask the leaders to designate more body-language cues to indicate other timbral, dynamic or rhythmic variations such as accents, three or four notes per beat, different tones to be played (open, muted, etc.), or any other musical variations.

• Combine with the 'hands' version to create something really crazy!

Discussion

• What was difficult/easy to follow? Why?

• Did leaders change their signals or add new ones? What were they?

• Did the leader group work well together?

• What would make this activity easier next time?

• Do the hoops need to be in a row? How else could they be arranged?

STITCH IN TIME

Music is everywhere—just look around! Students use the rhythms and patterns found in visual media to create their own drum ensembles. Ever wondered what a square sounds like? Now you can find out! This game helps students make musical connections to other disciplines outside (and inside) the arts, and can promote cultural awareness and appreciation for diversity.

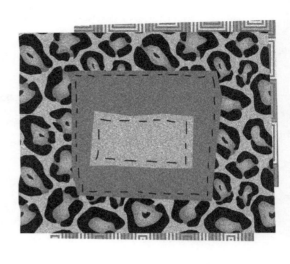

Time span: 20–30 minutes

Instruments: hand percussion, body percussion, or voice
Suggestions: A variety from the four timbre groups works best. If using one type of instrument (such as frame drums), encourage alternative techniques like scraping, tapping the shell, and muffling to produce different sounds.

Other materials: fabric, other visual media

Focus: creativity and composition, observing visual rhythms, appreciation of diversity, cultural pride, sharing

NS: 2 (performing), 4 (composing), 5 (reading), 6 (listening), 7 (evaluating), 8 (understanding relationships—arts) 9 (understanding relationships—culture)

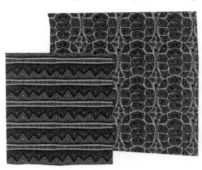

MI: visual/spatial, musical/rhythmic, mathematical/logical, naturalist

MT: leadership skills, impulse control, following multi-step directions, discrimination, cueing, modeling, attention span, communication skills

Preparation: Distribute small pieces of fabric (or photocopies) to all participants. Use fabric that has a recognizable pattern such as plaid, kente cloth, dots, stripes, etc. Participants may also be asked to bring fabric or patterns from home. Encourage students to bring a design that reflects their cultural heritage. Look to people's clothing and accessories for inspiration as well.

Process

1. Ask everyone to identify a pattern in his or her cloth. Point out that there are repeated patterns made up of different colors, light & dark lines, shapes, etc.

2. Ask students to choose an instrument (or use body or vocal percussion) and decide on at least two different sounds to represent the pattern in rhythm.

3. Allow a few minutes for the students to explore and develop their pattern(s).

4. Have everyone play his or her rhythmic pattern for the group and explain how it relates to the visual pattern.

   Example: "I snapped my fingers for the two triangles and clapped my hands for the squares."

Music Therapy Note: This activity may be too abstract for general music therapy applications; however, you can simplify it by supplying cloth or paper shapes and assigning rhythms or movements to the shapes (for example, square=4 beats, triangle=3 beats, circle=1 beat). Then the participants can put the shapes in various sequences (notation) and play the resulting rhythms.

Extension

- If the material has different sub-patterns that can be identified, have each person choose a different sub-pattern and play those groups of patterns all together.

- Have participants play patterns from other people's clothing (pants, skirt, shirt, etc.) to form an "ensemble" (note that we use the same term for someone's clothes as for a musical group). Discuss the concept of an ensemble with the group. (Definition of *ensemble*: at the same time; a group producing a single effect.)

- To encourage appreciation for cultural diversity and pride, ask students to bring a piece of traditional cloth from their background. Have the class use it to create music.

- Try the same exercises with photographs or drawings of train tracks, tiles, fences, orchards, brick walls & any images that have repeating patterns.

- Try it with items from nature such as leaves, ferns, wood grain, flowers, etc.

- Try playing patterns seen around the classroom or at home. Have students play them as–is, then arrange them to create their own compositions.

- Add or substitute movement or speech for instruments.

  Movement example: *"I flapped my arms like wings for the two triangles and crouched down for the squares."*

  Speech example: *"I said "Ti–Ki" for the two triangles and "Ta" for the squares."*

- Reverse the process by having some students first play their instruments, then have others draw patterns to represent what they heard.

- Have a student choose to play one of several patterns that everyone can see, but without letting anyone know which one. Ask the others if they think they know which pattern was played and why. Find out if they guessed right! Rotate players so everyone has a turn.

Discussion

- Are some patterns "louder" than others?

- What did you first notice about your pattern?

- Are some patterns more "angular," while others are more "fluid?" Would that affect your choice of instrument?

- Do certain sounds match certain colors or textures better than others? Which ones? Why?

- Can you see more rhythms & patterns in your surroundings than you could before we played this game? How would you represent them in sound or movement?

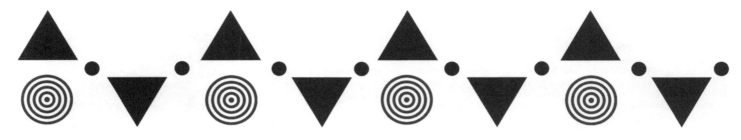

Pattern 1

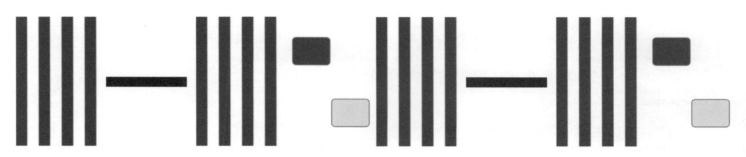

Pattern 2

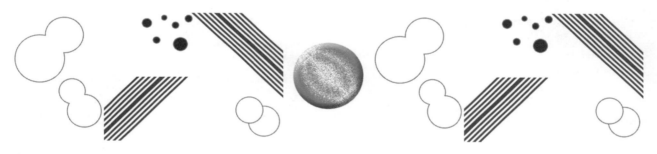

Pattern 3

Pattern 4

MUSIC PADS

Let's move! This game can be a wonderful launching pad for dance skills and illustrates the connection between movement and music. Students will develop leadership skills as they tap out the music. Always fun, and a great way to get in a little exercise![3]

Time span: 20–30 minutes

Instruments: drums and percussion
Suggestions: Provide a variety from the four main timbre groups (drums, wood, shakers, metal). If using similar instruments, create differences by using various sticks and mallets or techniques (short/long, high/low, hard/soft sounds).

Other materials: hoops or masking tape

Focus: associating movement with music, composing and arranging music, improvisation, creative movement, cooperation, spatial awareness, sharing, awareness of self and others, math/geometric concepts

NS: 2 (performing), 3 (improvising), 4 (composing), 6 (listening), 7 (evaluating)

MI: visual/spatial, musical/rhythmic, kinesthetic/bodily, interpersonal

MT: spatial awareness, group teamwork, attention span, following directions, impulse control, motor skills, non-verbal communication skills

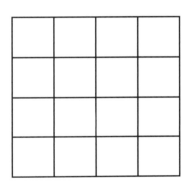

Your grid could have 4, 9, 16, or more pads!

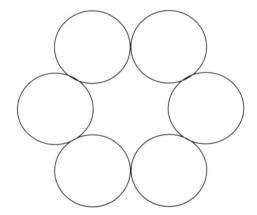

If using hoops, place them on the floor in a cluster.

Preparation: Create a number of "pads" with tape or hoops. If using tape, create a grid of squares on the floor. Make each square big enough so that someone can sit in it and play an instrument (about 2½ feet or 1 meter across). Place one instrument in each pad and have the group gather around the pads in a circle.

Process

1. Invite or choose students to sit in each pad. Have the rest of the students remain in the surrounding circle.

2. Explain that when someone visits a person's pad, they are to play their instrument as long as that visitor stays there, stopping when they leave.

3. Invite or choose students to walk around and visit pads, triggering the instrument in each (3–4 minutes).

4. Have the rest of the students play along with the pad instrument that best matches the one they have (rattle, drum, bell, etc.).

5. Have other students take turns being the visitor.

6. Ask everyone to remember which instruments are linked to each pad and move the students that are in the pads out to the circle, leaving the pads empty.

[3] Thanks to Sofia Lopez-Ibor, who presented the tape version of this game during my Level I Orff Schulwerk training at Mills College.

6. Choose a volunteer to move through the pads as the rest of the students play the sounds previously linked to each pad. Observe how they trigger musical sounds from the group. Do they step in rhythm? Do they try to visit all the pads? Do they use their hands or body in addition to their feet?

Extension

- Before placing the instruments inside the pads, ask participants to describe what they could be (windows, roads, a flower, etc).

- If using tape: Ask participants to imagine that the lines are streets. Have one of them drive his car to visit his friend on the other side of "town." Ask a volunteer to try and retrace his path. Ask everyone to drive their cars on the roads at the same time—CAREFULLY! No crashing or their cars will be "broken." See if they can get around by waiting at the intersections until the path is clear. Have everyone drive "home" (to the place they started).

- Choose two people to work together in the pads. See if they can coordinate their movements. Do they move together in rhythm? Are they using more than just their feet to trigger sounds?

Discussion

- Was it easy or difficult to follow the leaders? Why?
- Did anyone develop a new way to cue the music?
- Is there a place on the playground that would work well for this game? Where else?

ECHOES

HELLOOO HELLOOO HELLOOO HELLOOO...

This activity draws upon our natural instincts to repeat what we hear. It provides a great way to share musical ideas within the group and can be made either very easy or quite challenging. Students explore listening and responding to cues, create their own rhythms, take turns leading the group and expand their musical vocabulary through the sharing of ideas.

Time span: 10–20 minuntes

Instruments: drums and percussion, or body percussion
Suggestions: Provide a variety of instruments from the four main timbre groups (drums, wood, shakers, metal). Boomwhacker percussion tubes or individual Joia tubes also work well.

Focus: active listening, concentration, composing and arranging music, teamwork, improvisation, awareness of self and others

NS: 2 (performing), 3 (improvising), 4 (composing), 6 (listening), 7 (evaluating)

MI: musical/rhythmic, mathematical/logical, interpersonal

MT: cognitive skills reinforcement, self-esteem, creative self-expression (client leads), teamwork, leadership skills, modeling behaviors, impulse control, reality orientation, motor skills, sequencing

Preparation: Gather in a circle with instruments.

Process

Note: This exercise is an improvised round, sometimes referred to as a mini-canon.

1. Play a simple phrase (four or eight beats) for the group to echo.

Example: Simple Echo Activity

Leader plays A	Group echoes A	Leader plays B	Group echoes B	(etc…)

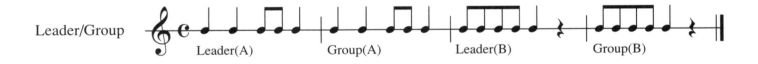

Leader/Group · Leader(A) · Group(A) · Leader(B) · Group(B)

To make it easier for the group to follow, use phrases that end on a strong beat such as beat 4 of a 4-beat measure.

4-Beat Rhythm Examples

1	+	2	+	3	+	4	+
Ta		Ta		Ti	Ti	Ta	
Ta		Ti	Ti	Ta		Ta	
Toe				Toe			
Ti	Ti	Ta		Toe			

8-Beat Rhythm Examples

1	+	2	+	3	+	4	+	5	+	6	+	7	+	8	+
Ti	Ti	Ta		Ti	Ti	Ta		Ti	Ti	Ta		Toe			
Toe				Toe				Ti	Ti	Ti	Ti	Ti	Ti	Ta	
Ta		Ta		Ta		Ta		Ti	Ti	Ta		Toe			
Ti	Ti	Ti	Ti	Ta		Ta		Ti	Ti	Ti	Ti	Toe			

2. Ask the group to echo as they have been doing, but instead of alternating turns, they will be playing one phrase while listening to the next one.

   Tip: Have the group play softly so they can hear the lead phrase. Have the leader play an instrument that can be easily heard such as woodblock or cowbell, or an an instrument no one else is playing so it is easy to distinguish. If the group is having trouble following or hearing the leader, adjust player positions, instruments, length of phrase, or playing volume to facilitate better conditions.

Example:

Leader plays A	Leader plays B	Leader plays C	Leader plays D
	Group echoes A, listens to B	Group echoes B, listens to C	Group echoes C, listens to D

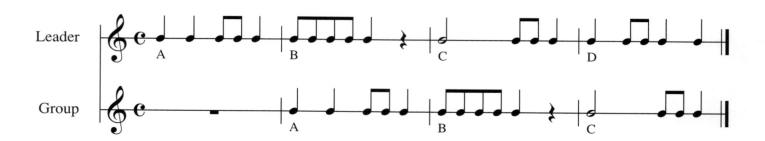

3. Invite or choose different leaders. Suggest varying the tempo and dynamics of the music.

Extension

Define a subgroup to echo the leader, and then have the rest of the group echo the subgroup.

Example:

1. The leader plays a phrase.
2. The leader's phrase is echoed by all the wood instruments.
3. The rest of the group echoes the wood instruments.

In this configuration, there are three different rhythms going on at once and each player must maintain enough focus not only to play their current rhythm, but to listen for the next one as well. If echoing in timbre groups is difficult, it may help to divide the group in half, having one half echo the leader and the other half echo the first half. Experiment with various subgroups such as boys/ girls, instrument types, pitch, etc.

Example:

Leader plays A	Leader plays B	Leader plays C	Leader plays D
Group 1 listens to leader play A	Group 1 echoes A, listens to Leader play B	Group 1 echoes B, listens to Leader play C	Group 1 echoes C, listens to Leader play D
	Group 2 listens to Group 1 play A	Group 2 echoes A, listens to Group 1 play B	Group 2 echoes B, listens to Group 1 play C

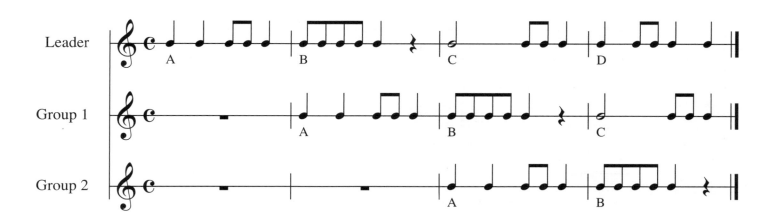

Note: This activity can be challenging, but if achieved cannot only produce interesting music, but may provide a great sense of teamwork and accomplishment for the entire group. This structure affords many opportunities for building collaborative skills and creative thinking.

Discussion

- What kinds of phrases or rhythms were easiest to echo? Why?
- How did it feel to have to play and listen at the same time?
- Where did you focus your attention?
- Did this way of listening change your relationship with the people next to you?

Multiple Intelligence Use Chart

Use this chart to find the right game(s) for your programs. In many instances, the same game may fall under more than one related category.

	Rhythmic			Verbal	Mathematical	Visual	Kinesthetic	Interpersonal	Intrapersonal	Naturalist
	Involves a little rhythm	Involves some rhythm	Involves a lot of rhythm							
Rain	•			•						•
Drum Tales	•			•				•	•	•
Rumble Ball	•					•	•			
Foley	•	•	•			•	•	•		•
Rhythmaze	•	•			•	•	•		•	
Drum Call		•	•	•	•			•		
Secret Song		•		•				•		
Orbit		•			•			•		•
Have a Ball		•		•		•		•		
Let's All Play Our Drum		•	•	•	•		•			
Sound Machine			•			•		•		
Pieces of Eight			•		•			•		
Rhythmasize Your Name			•	•				•		
Signals: Hands			•		•	•	•	•		
Signals: Feet			•		•	•	•	•		
Stitch in Time			•		•	•				•
Music Pads	•	•	•			•	•	•		
Echos		•	•		•			•		

Drum Circle Music Cards

I created these cards for groups who wish to learn about rhythms and how different rhythms can fit together in different ways. They're as simple to use as building blocks, and just as flexible.

Music educators and facilitators are often looking for ways to address the various learning styles of their groups. Western and rhythm-box notation offers a linear perspective of time and rhythmic events that seems to work for most people, especially those who favor text-based methods of communicating ideas and concepts. But rhythms can also be thought of as *cycles*, which may take on the circular shape of a clock or wheel. This approach usually appeals to people who favor visual/spatial learning.

What Is a Drum Circle Music Card?

A Rhythm Circle Card contains a circular representation of a rhythmic phrase.

There are five different rhythm cards and a blank "master" that you can use to create your own cards.

How to Read a Drum Circle Music Card

The points at the top, bottom, left, and right of the circle represent primary beats.

The "corners" represent upbeats.

Black dots represent sounds.

White dots represent rests.

The arrow indicates the orientation of the card.

In this example, the resulting rhythm is as follows:

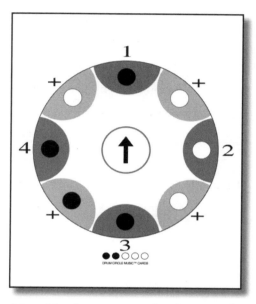

Note: Numbers appear in this diagram only, not on the cards.

1	+	2	+	3	+	4	+
•				•	•	•	

How to Use Drum Circle Music Cards

1. Make copies of the cards and pass them out to your group. You may wish to use sets of colored paper (one color for each rhythm) to make the cards easy to distinguish.

   Tip: You don't need a card for each participant. Provide them for small groups of people who can all read off the same card.

2. Explain the concept of Drum Circle Music Cards to the group, or let them figure it out on their own!

Key Concept

Each card is like an analog clock face, where 12 o'clock is beat **1**, 3 o'clock is beat **2**, 6 o'clock is beat **3**, and 9 o'clock is beat **4**. It may help to have participants point to the beats on the card as you count out loud from one to four.

3. Assign sounds to the cards.

   Using body percussion: Assign different body percussion sounds to each card, or use the master card to create versions with different symbols that mix body percussion sounds on each card.

   Using vocal sounds: Same as above, but using vocal sounds.

   Using drums: Assign a different timbre group to each card, or use the master card to make cards that indicate different types of sounds (such as low and high).

4. Each card may be rotated 90, 180 or 270 degrees to produce new rhythms.

5. Cards can be read both forwards and backwards.

6. Groups may decide what kinds of sounds they want the dots to represent.

Example Activity: Timber Groups

- Start the low drums playing card no. 1.
- Start the high drums on card no. 2.
- Start the wood sounds on card no. 3.
- Start the shakers & rattles on card no. 4.
- Start the metal sounds on card no. 5.
- Pause the music (or one group) and have each group rotate their card 90, 180, or 270 degrees, or keep it where it is. Experiment with various combinations and discuss how rotating the cards changed the feel of the music.

Example Activity: Card Sharing

- Have four students gather around one card, one at each side.
- Have each student play the rhythm they see (from their perspective).
- Try the above with a mix of body percussion, vocal sounds and/or instruments.

Example Activity: Create and Compare

- Distribute copies of the master card to the students. Have each create his or her own rhythm by filling in dots.
- Provide a steady pulse and have each student clap his or her rhythm.
- Ask students to form same-rhythm groups by clapping their rhythms and moving into groups (without talking).
- Orchestrate the patterns using vocal percussion, body percussion, instruments, or a combination of these.

    Bonus: Challenge students to see if the rhythms of any of the groups would be the same if one of the cards was rotated 90, 180, or 260 degrees. (The rhythm pattern would be the same starting on a different beat.)

Drum Circle Music Cards provide a flexible way to teach rhythms and teamwork, develop visual learning skills, and illustrate mathematical and geometric concepts. They can also lead to cross-curricular discussions that relate to orbits, planets, cycles, rotation, and other subjects that may help to "round out" a learning experience.

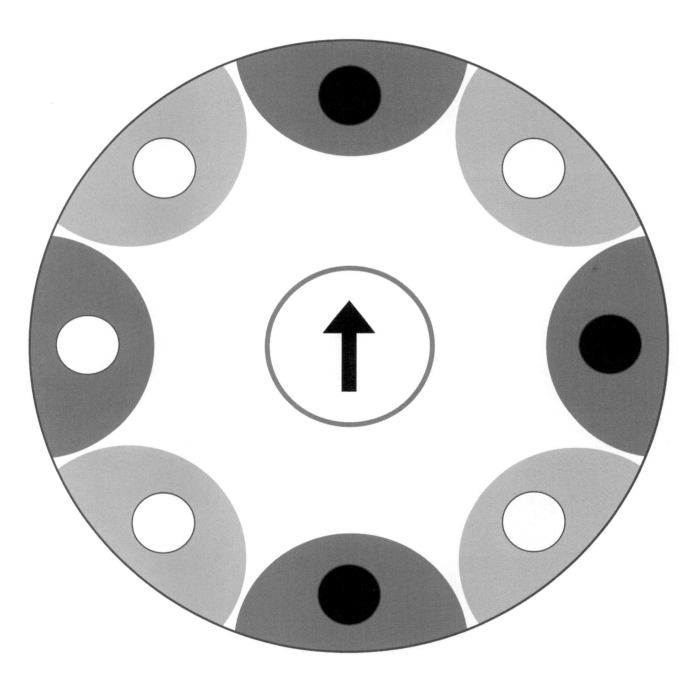

DRUM CIRCLE MUSIC™ CARDS

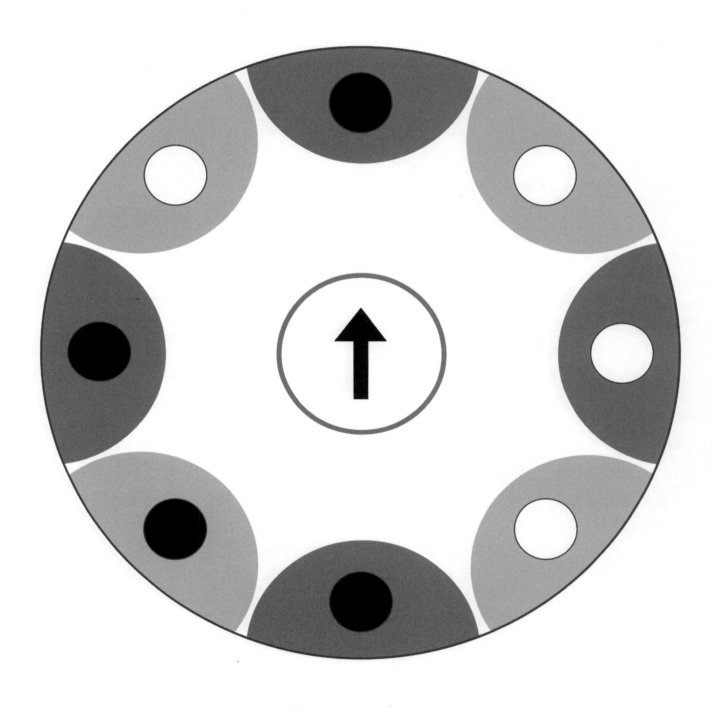

DRUM CIRCLE MUSIC™ CARDS

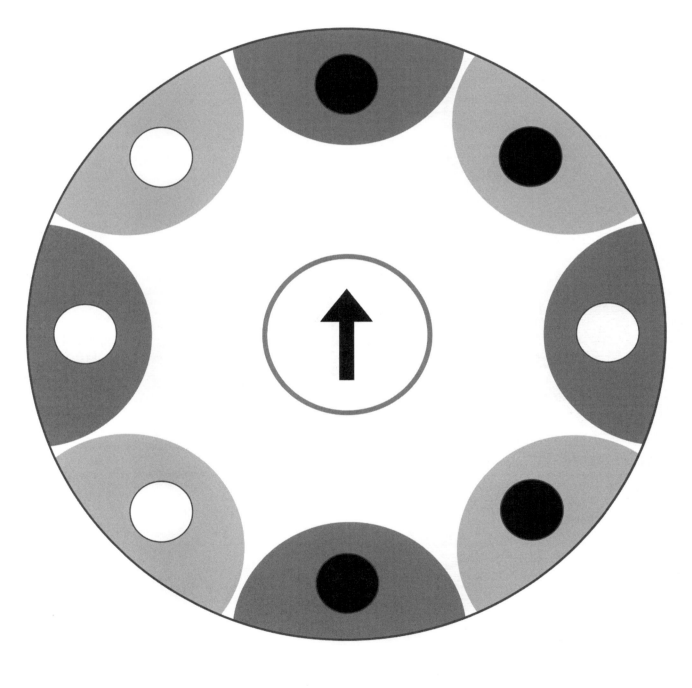

DRUM CIRCLE MUSIC™ CARDS

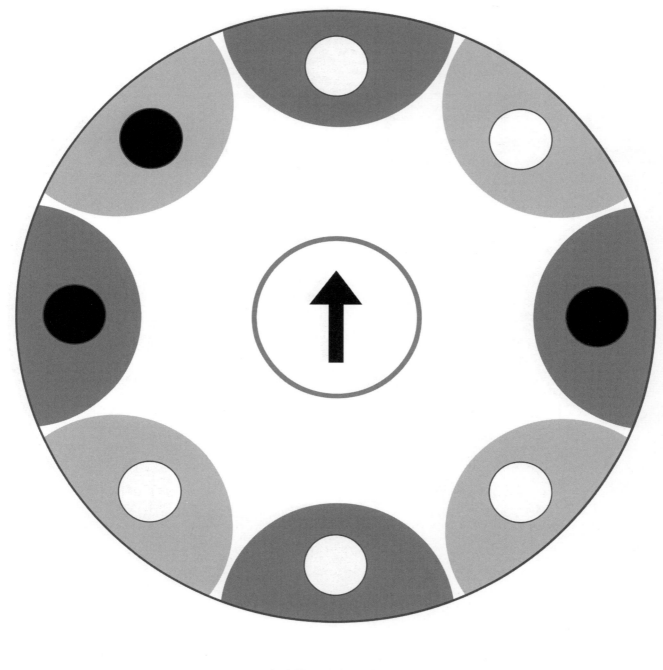

DRUM CIRCLE MUSIC™ CARDS

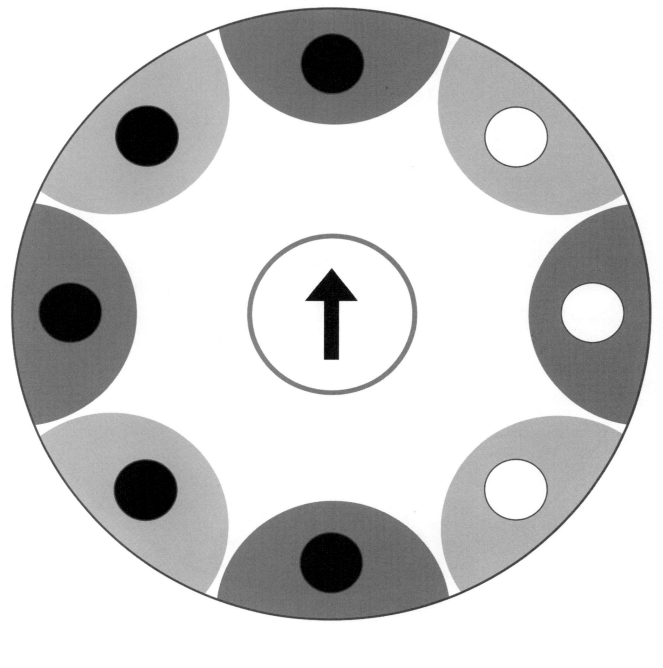

DRUM CIRCLE MUSIC™ CARDS

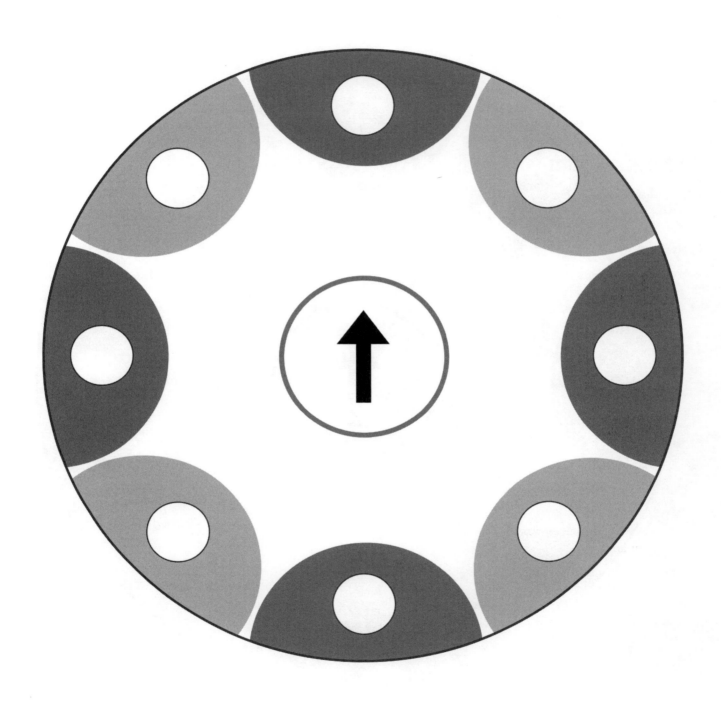

DRUM CIRCLE MUSIC™ CARDS

Making Your Own Instruments

Many percussion instruments simply started off as ordinary or "found" objects such as boxes, cans, logs, tubes and whatever else you could find out in the shed. (Don't even get me started in the kitchen!) Over the years, many of those items were refined and became "real" instruments, but "junk" percussion is still alive and well today. One of my favorite instruments is a metal trashcan! I think it sounds great, and I've used it on several recordings.

The following instruments can be made quite easily as home or school projects for little or no money. Make all of them and have a complete drum circle kit for your family or classroom! Prices are estimates. Personal experience may vary.

Note: Always be sure to wear the proper safety equipment when operating power tools such as drills and saws, or when using sharp objects such as utility knifes.

Water Jug Drum

Estimated time to build: 1 hour

Adult supervision required

Materials:

• One 5-gallon water jug. Cost: $5–8.
Specialty water stores and some grocery stores sell varieties of water jugs, all with their own unique sound. Experiment and find the jug you like the best.

• 4 to 5 feet of 1/2-inch rope for the strap. Cost: $1–3.
Almost any hardware store has an assortment of rope. Cotton rope is inexpensive and comfortable.

Tools:

• Sharp utility knife (razor blade)

• Electric drill with 1/2-inch bit

• Felt-tip marker

Process:

1. Make a circle on the opening side (top) of the jug with a felt marker. Mark around the circumference so when you make your cut, the entire spout and shoulder is gone and the remaining part is a basic cylinder.

2. Carefully and slowly cut along your line. This step may require assistance or supervision depending on how thick the plastic is. If necessary, sand, file or cut the edge so there are no sharp spots.

3. For the strap, mark two holes with a marker on the side of the jug three inches from the bottom (playing surface) and three inches apart. Carefully and thoroughly drill the holes out with a 1/2-inch bit.

4. Thread the rope through one hole and out the other. Tie this strap loosely around your waist so the drum hangs comfortably in between your thighs, and cut off any excess rope.

Play: Strap on the drum and play the top (originally the bottom of the jug) with the fingers, bundled sticks (RUTEs) or soft mallets.

Square Frame Drum

Square frame drums are commonly found in Western Europe, West Africa and Persian-Arabic cultures. They are usually held in one hand and played with the other.

Estimated time to build: 1 hour

Materials:

• One 4-foot-long piece of 2-inch x 2-inch wood.   Cost: $3–6.
Pine wood is cheap and it works fine. Available at most hardware stores.

• Clear plastic packing tape. Cost: $3–5 per roll.
Available at most hardware or craft stores.

Tools:

• Hand saw and miter box
• Wood glue
• Small hammer
• Eight 2-inch finishing nails

Process:

1. Carefully cut wood into four pieces that are 8 inches long.

2. Arrange cut pieces so they construct a solid square. It is important that each piece is flush with the others and that all are even and flat.

3. Sparingly use wood glue at contact points, and then carefully hammer nails (2) at the ends of pieces so that all pieces are joined. Let stand overnight or until the glue is dry.

4. Starting from one end of the square, wrap the tape as tightly as possible around the frame. You should wrap so the tape is not quite straight (overlapping as you go), to make a continuous layer from one side of the square to the opposite side without cutting the tape. The tape should barely overlap the previous pass so there are no holes in the layer.

5. Turn the square 90 degrees and repeat step 4 to make two layers of tape that are perpendicular to each other. Remember to tape as tightly as possible. When the second layer is done, be sure the end of the tape is secure on one of the sides of the frame.

Note: The tape will stretch and cause the drum to become lower-pitched over time. To make your drum's tone last longer, play gently with your hands or with a soft mallet.

Play: Hold the frame of the instrument as shown and strike the head with your fingers or with a soft mallet (either purchased or made from objects found around the home or classroom).

Shakers

Estimated time to build: 10 to 20 minutes

Materials:

- Plastic bottles, tin cans, cardboard/PVC tube
- Rice, small beads, un-popped popcorn, small dried beans, or BBs
- Duct tape. Cost: $2–4 per roll.
- Glue (optional)
- Decorative cloth or paper (optional)

Tools:

- Scissors

Process:

1. Fill the desired container to approximately one-eighth of its capacity with the desired filler. Rice works well in plastic bottles and cardboard tubes, while the other fillers are louder and sound best in metal cans and PVC tubing.

2. Cover with a lid. If no lid is available, use the duct tape to cover exposed holes. A circular piece of cardboard that is the same size as the diameter of the opening may be taped into place to keep the filler in.

3. Cut decorative cloth or paper and glue onto the container.

Play: Hold as shown and shake away!

Sistrum

Sistrums are commonly found in Egyptian and West African countries. They are one of the oldest types of percussion instruments, dating back to at least 2500 B.C., and were often played in ceremonies and rituals.

Estimated time to build: 1 to 1½ hours

Requires light adult supervision

Materials:

- 30-inch piece of accent molding or thin wood stripping (½-inch or less in width). Cost: $3–5.
- 15 to 18 bottle caps. Cost: free.
- Light-weight picture hanging wire. Cost: $1.
- String (similar to kite string). Cost: $2–3.

Tools:

- Small hand saw
- Hammer
- 1 large nail
- Scissors
- Glue (wood glue is best)

Process:

1. Cut wood stripping into two pieces 10 inches long and two pieces 5 inches long.

2. Arrange the pieces to construct a rectangle with ½ inch overhang on each side.

3. Glue at points of contact in the corners and let dry. Apply pressure while drying.

4. Tightly wrap and tie the corners with string to strengthen the frame.

5. Punch holes in the center of the bottle caps with the hammer and nail, then carefully flatten the caps with the hammer on a hard surface. (*Option: For a brighter tone, remove the plastic liner in the caps before you flatten them.*)

6. Cut three 8-inch long pieces of picture hanging wire. Tie one end of each wire to one of the longer sides of the rectangle, keeping them about two inches apart.

7. String through five to six bottle caps on each of the wires.

8. Tightly tie the loose end of each wire to the other side of the rectangle.

Play: Hold and play the sistrum like a shaker.

Bundled "Puili" Sticks

Puili (poo–EE–lee) sticks are a Hawaiian instrument used in traditional dance. They are usually made from sections of bamboo that are cut lengthwise to form many small slats that rattle together when struck.

Estimated time to build: 20 to 30 minutes

Materials:

• 12 to 16 thin bamboo garden stakes (available at most home improvement centers). Cost: $5–8.

• Masking or duct tape. Cost: $1–2 per roll.

• 3 feet of 1/8-inch thick cotton rope. Cost: $2.

Tools:

• Saw

• Scissors

Process:

1. Cut the stakes to 22 inches long.

2. Tape groups of 6 to 8 stakes together about 4 inches from one end.

3. Wrap about 6 inches of rope around one end to form a handle. Secure the end of the rope with a knot or tape.

Play: Hold the sticks by the handles and strike them together or on the floor.

Found Instruments

(stuff that's layin' around just waitin' to be played)

Rocks (Clack 'em together.)

Sticks (Hit 'em together or use 'em on other stuff.)

Cans (Play 'em with your fingers or with sticks.)

Pots & Pans (Hit 'em with plastic or wood so ya don't make dents.)

Buckets (Flip 'em over and go for it.)

Cardboard Boxes (Good sound—short lifespan.)

Training Programs

Drum Circle Music certification training programs are designed around Kalani's innovative and successful facilitation techniques and strategies. They provide participants with a dynamic learning environment that pulsates with energy, information and fun!

An abundance of useful activities and drum circle games are presented in a setting of exploration and creative learning. Instructor and peer feedback help participants gain valuable insights into their potential and empower them to grow on many levels.

Benefits of Participation

- Play and learn about instruments that are used in drum circles
- Develop facilitation techniques, strategies and presentation skills
- Learn how to use the drum circle format in your profession
- Gain valuable business tools, resources and feedback
- Develop your presentation, leadership and "followership" skills
- Improve your sense of rhythm and drumming techniques
- Discover how to plan, organize, promote and present a rhythm-based event

Who Should Attend?

- Music teachers and school teachers
- Therapists and social workers
- Health care providers
- Recreation activity directors
- Drum circle facilitators
- Anyone who loves music and people

Professional Standards

If you are a music educator or music therapist, you will find that Drum Circle Music supports the goals and standards of your profession and provides useful activities that can easily be incorporated into your work. If you are new to drum circles or even to music, DCM will provide you with everything you need to facilitate group music making with confidence. If you are an experienced drum circle facilitator, you will find many valuable resources that will help you take your art to the next level and beyond.

Our Mission

The mission of Kalani Music is to develop relevant and valuable resources and technologies, as well as professional development opportunities, that meet or exceed the current professional standards of music educators, music therapists and others in related professions. We are committed to the growth and success of each participant.

Where Can I Learn More?

You can find useful information on the Drum Circle Music website, **DrumCircleMusic.com**. You'll find downloads, articles, and other resources, and you can find out how to attend one of our training programs.

Do you have questions or stories to share with other DCM facilitators? Join the Drum Circle Music user group by sending an e-mail to **Drum_Circle_Music-subscribe@yahoogroups.com**, or you can visit the group site at **http://launch.groups.yahoo.com/group/Drum_Circle_Music/**.

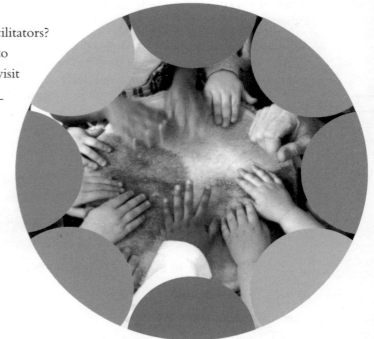

Resources

Kalanimusic.com Kalani's website.

Drumlesson.com On-line lessons, instrument encyclopedia, artist interviews, member forums.

Drumcamp.com Music education programs, world drumming and dance.

Tocapercussion.com Toca Percussion Instruments website for drums and percussion.

LPMusic.com Latin Percussion website for drums and percussion.

Peripole.com Orff instruments and world percussion for the classroom.

Recreationalmusic.com Connect with other players, find a drum jam, keep an on-line drumming journal.